THE UPROOTED

Displacement Resettlement Development

THE UPROOTED

DISPLACEMENT RESETTLEMENT DEVELOPMENT

Edited by

V. Sudarsen and M.A. Kalam

GYAN

Published by

GYAN

Gyan Publishing House
5, Ansari Road
Daryaganj, New Delhi-110002
Phone: 011-47034999, 9811692060
E-mail: books@gyanbooks.com

Distribution Network
gyanbooks.com
India, USA, Canada, UK, Australia, France

ISBN: 978-81-212-0414-9 (HB)
First Published, 1990

Printed at: Gyan Press, Delhi.

The Uprooted: Development, Displacement and Resettlement
Author: V. Sudarsen; M.A. Kalam

Acknowledgements

This volume is an outcome of the National Seminar on "The Developmental Process and the Problems of Rehabilitation and Relocation of the Uprooted" held in March, 1989 at Madras University. The seminar was sponsored by University Grants Commission and Indian Council of Social Science Research. We thank both these agencies for the financial support.

In an effort to bring out this volume soon after the seminar, we fixed a very stringent deadline for the submission of the revised version of the paper to the authors. In spite of the short time given to them, all the authors responded favourably to our request and submitted the papers almost sticking to the deadline given. We are very happy and thankful to the contributors for the keen interest they have shown in this effort.

The tedious process of proof-reading the manuscript was ungrudgingly undertaken by Mr. D. Venkatesan—We are very grateful to him. Mr. J. Sekhar did a marvellous job of typing the manuscript in a short time and we thank him for the neat job done.

We also express our sincere thanks for the publishers M/s Gian Publishing House, New Delhi 110002 for undertaking the publication and for bringing out the volume in a short time.

V. Sudarsen M.A. Kalam

Contributors

Andre Beteille	Department of Sociology Delhi School of Economics Delhi University Delhi-110007
N. Subba Reddy	Centre for Economic and Social Studies, Nizamia Observatory Complex Begumpet, Hyderabad-500 016
V. Suryanarayan	Centre for South and Southeast Asian Studies University of Madras, Madras—600 005
D. Venkatesan	Department of Anthropology University of Madras Madras—600 005
V. Sudarsen	Department of Anthropology University of Madras Madras—600 005
N.K. Behura	Department of Anthropology Utkal University Vani Vihar Bhubaneswar-751 004 (Orissa)
V. Gangadhar	Department of Social Anthropology Sri Venkateswara University Tirupati-517 502 (A.P.)

D. Padmavathi	Centre for Women Development Studies Mahila University Tirupati (A.P.)
B.M. Mukherjee	Department of Anthropology Manipur University Canchipur-Imphal 795003 (Manipur)
P. Sudhakara Reddy	Department of Social Anthropology, S.V. University Tirupati—517 502 (A.P.) Madras—600 005
I. Udaya Bhaskara Reddy	Unit for Urban Studies Tata Institute of Social Sciences Sion-Trombay Road, Deonar Bombay--400 088
R. Yathiraj Kumar	Department of Anthropology Andhra University Waltair-530 003 (A.P.)
B.L. Joshi	Department of Sociology Marathwada University Aurangabad (Maharashtra)
M.A. Kalam	Department of Anthropology University of Madras Madras-600005
R. Siva Prasad	Om Consultants (India) Pvt. Ltd. P.B. 356 Malleswaram Bangalore (Karnataka)
A. Xavier Raj	Department of Anthropology University of Madras Madras—600 005
Satwant Kaur	Department of Anthropology University of Madras Madras—600 005

Contents

Introduction

V. Sudarsen and M.A. Kalam

I

The process of modernization and industrialization started as a means of establishing economic independence in many third world countries as a consequence of lop-sided growth during the imperialist rule. In India too, this process of industrialization started with the very First Five-Year Plan. In addition to the establishment of core industries, India also witnessed the establishment of educational and research institutions at the national level. As a part of the planned development several irrigation and multipurpose projects were planned and executed. This planned development was certainly a progressive step leading towards India's self-reliance in the fields of science, technology and industry.

These developmental projects certainly were intended for the benefit of the common citizens of India. However, the benefits that accrued from these developmental projects are by no means uniform. There is always a section of the society which is adversely affected by the execution of the developmental projects. Thus, though the establishment of industries, laboratories, irrigation projects, *etc.*, is a step forward, at the national level, at a micro level all these developmental projects have uprooted several groups of people from their traditional moorings. The rehabilitation and relocation of such groups of people requires a definite policy stand on the part of the Government and cannot be treated in a *laissez-faire* manner.

Rehabilitation and relocation are, primarily, human problems. Basically there are economic questions entangled with rehabilitation and a wide range of socio-cultural and psychological problems connected to the whole question of rehabilitation and relocation. It is obvious that the suffering from an economic point of view is not equal to all the uprooted people. There are certain sections of the uprooted like the agricultural labourers, marginal farmers, *etc.* who are more vulnerable to the sufferings as a consequence of their being uprooted.

The magnitude of the problem of rehabilitation can be gauged from the fact that if all the projects envisaged on Narmada valley are implemented about a million people have to be rehabilitated. This project involves some 3000 dams of various sizes. Similarly for establishing National Testing Range (NTR) at Baliapal in Orissa, evacuation of about one lakh people in about 130 villages covering an area of 160 sq. kms was thought to be necessary. But ultimately the area of evacuation was brought down to 102 sq. kms, necessitating 45,000 people in 54 villages to be rehabilitated. These figures do not take into account those who are seasonally and indirectly employed in this area. In addition, the official figures on Baliapal do not take into account the fishermen families which are about 1500 in number, spread over 27 villages (AIFOFDR, 1986).

As soon as Government of India announced the establishment of NTR in 1985, there was a spontaneous resistance movement from the people who are going to be uprooted. Perhaps as an attempt at pacifying the people, Government of India announced an elaborate plan of rehabilitation and compensation worth Rs. 127 crores (Central Government Report, 1986). If the people are agitated and pessimistic about rehabilitation programmes, they do so with good reason. Out of the 30,000 people rendered homeless by the Rengali project twelve years ago, about 20,000 are yet to be rehabilitated (Nair, 1987).

In the garb of National Interest and National Development, projects and plans are executed ; whose interests do they really serve ? This is a crucial question since while implementing each of these projects the proportion of the tribal and other weaker sections among the uprooted is considerable. There are two specific points which need attention in this context. One is the fact that in the whole process of rehabilitation the groups referred above are the most severely affected. Most of the landless agricultural labourers and marginal farmers come from these groups. Most of these tribals and other small farmers, moreover, were traditionally cultivating the lands for a very long time but without any landholding documents. The State itself considers them, while evacuating, as "encroachers" without taking into due consideration their longstanding affinity with the land. Just to illustrate this point one can glean through the Government of India's policy of land acquisition for NTR. Out of the 21,000 acres required for the range, 11,000 acres was considered "encroached" by local farmers and no compensation was paid for that land.

The second point which requires a greater amount of consideration is the fact that the rehabilitation plans try to keep the *status-quo* in terms of economic relations in the relocated context. Keeping in view the fact that most of the times rehabilitation is a forced and planned change, one wonders why the rehabilitation plan should not include a more equitable distribution of land and other economic assets amongst the evictees.

II

The environmental question, of late, is no more an academic one but is a people's concern. People are reacting sharply to the official planners' analysis of cost-benefit assessments ; take the question of China's Yangtze and, nearer home, India's Narmada project. A realistic assessment of the environmental imperatives and the developmental goals is an absolute necessity, more so in the developing world. If the Chinese government is compelled to put off its massive project, Yangtze project, till 1996 and having a second look at the environmental aspects, it is with good reason. The Indian experience in this regard, whether in Orissa or in Tamil Nadu and whether it is the National Testing Range or an Atomic Nuclear Reactor, should be taken seriously of while planning and implementing the plans.

The concept of sustainable development is gaining ground all over the world. The realization in practice of this concept requires the full support of the governments and policy planners ; when we say this, we are fully aware of the linkages between the social system in India and the political institution. The nexus between the groups with vested interests bent upon exploiting the natural resources *at any cost* and the political power bases can be countered only by people's participation. If the majority of People of India opt for "lower standards of living with few...risks" than "higher standards but with greater risk...(*The Hindu*, May 18, 1989), it only means that there is a need to have a closer look at our developmental priorities.

These and a host of other questions beg our attention. A stock-taking of the problems involved in rehabilitation due to whatever programme or project is the immediate need.

The present volume is the outcome of a seminar on the theme of 'Developmental Process and the Problems of Rehabilitation and Relocation of the Uprooted' held on 13th and 14th of March, 1989 at Madras University. The seminar generated extensive empirical-data from various parts of the country and there was considerable discussion on various points connected to the main theme.

As we were planning to organize the seminar, we realized that the problem of rehabilitation is not just a consequence of the developmental projects alone. But another important reason for uprooting people is political. Though the reason is different, the latter also causes all the human suffering and agony as does the former. That was precisely the reason why we made the framework of this seminar more broad-based.

III

This volume includes papers presented at the seminar. We have classified the papers in terms of the main thrust of the paper. The first section includes papers on the rehabilitation programmes as a consequence to political process. Section two contains various studies concerning the rehabilitation programmes as a consequence of developmental projects. These papers cover several facets of the problem of rehabilitation from different parts of India, while the third section includes those papers which are basically conceptual in nature and concern the policy planning aspect of the rehabilitation problem.

REFERENCES

AIFOFDR (All-India Federation of Organisations for Democratic Rights)
(1986) *People* vs *Baliapal Missile Base.*

Central Government Report
(1986) National Testing Range—Baliapal.

NAIR, V. (1987) Resistance unto Death against the Establishment of Baliapal Missile Test Range. *Ananda Bazaar Patrika.* 9 May. Calcutta.

The Hindu. (1989) Far from apathetic (Editiorial), May 18.

Inaugural Speech

Prof. Andre Beteille*

Let me begin by saying that I am really very happy being here with you and to associate myself with the National Seminar as well as the two lectures being organised in connection with the 125th birth anniversary of late L.K. Ananthakrishna Iyer. Having said that and having expressed my gratitude for the distinction that has been conferred on me by inviting me to inaugurate the seminar, let me say that I feel a little apprehensive about performing that kind of role. In our country it is the customary practice to get some dignitary to inaugurate anything, absolutely anything including an academic seminar. And I have always felt uneasy about that because these dignitaries usually arrive late, leave early and have very little to say. And from that point of view you have done well to choose a working anthropologist who is like one of you to inaugurate this function. On the other hand, I must say that inaugurating seminars like everything else requires some experience, that I have no experience whatsoever in playing this role and therefore I was somewhat nervous and uneasy about what has been described as my address. Secondly, there is a very particular reason why I feel even more uneasy

* Dept. of Sociology, Delhi School of Economics, Delhi University, Delhi 110007.

about speaking for any length of time on this occasion ; because I have to perform very soon afterwards with regards to my two L.K. Ananthakrishna Iyer Memorial lectures, and I do not wish to drive away the audience, which I hope will remain behind to listen to the two lectures which I have come here primarily to deliver.

I would, nevertheless, like to recall my association with Tamil Nadu. In the very beginning of my professional career I decided to do my fieldwork in the Tanjore district. In those days I must confess I felt rather uneasy about visiting the University. I was so pre-occupied with getting to the village. So this in fact is the first occasion on which I find myself in this very distinguished University. I am really very happy to be here and to say a few words on this occasion when you are going to begin your deliberations on this very important topic. When I look back to the period when I first came to Madras on the way to Tanjore, I find that Social Anthropology and Sociology, and I always regarded these two disciplines to be as closely related as to be in one sense, in a broader sense, to be one and the same. When I look back on these disciplines in those years, 1961-62, I find that many changes have come about in Sociology and Social Anthropology, particularly in Social Anthropology because of what Social Anthropologists do today is in many ways rather different from what we were trying to do in the late fifties and the early sixties. But this is the attitude ; I am greatly impressed by the many advances that have been made in this discipline. But I would also like to remind you of some of the strengths of the older discipline so that one does not lose sight of those strengths in developing into newer areas and in formulating new models and new approaches and solutions to those problems. I do wish to emphasize the fact that in a sense the strengths of the old discipline of anthropology are best exemplified indeed by the first generation of Indian anthropologists. The founding father of Indian anthropology, L.K. Ananthakrishna Iyer, who as you know was associated with Madras University but then later during a very long part of his career also with the University of Calcutta. I think also of the late S.C. Roy who was along with the late L.K. Ananthakrishna Iyer one of the pioneers of the discipline of anthropology.

They were not trained anthropologists in the sense that they did not have teachers in the discipline of anthropology as we have. They created the discipline of anthropology and they mostly worked with rusted tools ; their tools were not very refined and not very sophisticated. Younger generation of anthropologists working today operate with tools, with techniques, with methods which are rather more economic rather more sophisticated. But at the same time I think these anthropologists had certain strengths and we must not lose sight of their strengths. I think their work was very firmly grounded in an empirical tradition and I believe that this grounding in fieldwork in the empirical tradition is really what gives to anthropology its permanent garb. Many things come and go in anthropology, there are many factions in anthropology and sociology as you know in all other disciplines ; if there is something really permanent, something really enduring about the discipline of Sociology and Social Anthropology, I think that is its grounding in the empirical realities and its solid foundations in the empirical field and empirical fieldwork in a variety of different communities, because our country, our society and culture is very highly diversified. I often tell my own students that the comparative method is the heart and soul of Sociology or Social Anthropology. I would like to recall the words of Durkheim who said that the comparative method is not a special branch of Sociology, it is Sociology itself. And I think the same applies to Social Anthropology. Now, how does one apply the comparative method ? I was having a look at the titles of the various papers that are going to be presented in this seminar. What impressed me most about these papers is the wide range of experiences that are covered by the papers. And that is really very very important. There are several ways in which one can apply the comparative method to the study of human society and culture. One of course is to go to different countries and study societies and cultures in all the different countries of the world. For a variety of different reasons this has not been very easy for us in India, mainly for lack of resources as well as for other reasons. Most Indian Sociologists and Social Anthropologists have been confined to doing fieldwork in India. A few have gone to neighbouring countries and I feel the more this is done the more this kind of work is extended, the better it is for the development of Sociology and Social Anthropology not only in India but the world over. But even without that I think there is enormous scope for the application of comparative method while remaining within India itself. We should take advantage of the fact that India is a very very large country and the scope for comparison within India itself is enormous.

I am eternally grateful to my then supervisor, and mentor Prof. M.N. Srinivas, for forcing me, literally forcing me out of Delhi out of West, Bengal to come to Tamil Nadu to work in an area which I had never known before. That is one thing for which I remain very very grateful to Prof. Srinivas. He said 'I know that you will find it very difficult at first and I know you will curse me but in the end you will be grateful that I persuaded you to do this'. And whenever I find the occasion and the opportunity I will try to send my own students out as far afield as possible. I think that every Indian Sociologist or Social Anthropologist must have the experience of at least doing one piece of fieldwork in a part of the country other than his own. And I have no doubt whatsoever that this experience will greatly enrich his understanding of his own part of the country. Yes, I did later on go back to West Bengal. And when I went back to West Bengal carrying with me the experience of my fieldwork in Tanjore district I think I was able to see West Bengal in a much larger perspective which would not have been possible, if I had started and ended my field research in West Bengal ; and I think that is a permanent gain which one gets by being an anthropologist and by taking a look at other areas, at other cultures than one's own. It loosens the smugness with which one looks at the world and I think in the broader sense that is the kind of educational value of Social Anthropology and Comparative Sociology—that it shakes up your complete system. It makes you realise that the customs to which you are accustomed from childhood are not the only customs, there are alternative ways of living, there are alternative designs of living and you must come to understand and appreciate the full range of the ways of living which human beings have devised in different parts of the world at different historical epochs. When I teach courses in Comparative Sociology to my students I often begin by quoting to them an old Chinese proverb which says, 'when I carefully consider the curious habits of gods I am content to conceive that man is a superior animal. When I consider the curious habits of man I confess my frienc I am puzzled'. That is, when we look at the peculiarities of other people we think we are superior but looking at the peculiarities of other people should train us to look at our own peculiarities and then we realise that we are not all that superior after all. I think that is a great educative value of Anthropology and Comparative Sociology. And one of the things that has impressed me greatly by the development in our discipline over the last 25 years is the wide range of topics to which the younger generation of sociologists and social anthropologists have addressed themselves. If I have one unhappiness about the development of Sociology and Social Anthropology over the 25 or 30 years it is this that in one sense these anthropologists and sociologists have become very conservative ; each one studies the society or culture of his own area. If he is from Orissa he is quite satisfied to start his fieldwork in Orissa and ends it there. If he is from West Bengal he starts his fieldwork in West Bengal and ends it there. If he is from Tamil Nadu he starts his fieldwork and ends it there. I do not say there are no exceptions. There are exceptions. But I wish that the exceptions would be many many more. And that a law could be established whereby a young anthropologist starts his fieldwork in an area other than where he comes from. Firstly, because when one is young it is easier to adjust oneself to a different mode of livelihood. Anthropological fieldwork is no joke. You not only have to adjust yourself, adapt yourself to materially very different circumstances, different food, different environment, different climate, but emotionally, morally you have to adjust yourself to different climates and that takes a lot of doing. Therefore I feel the sooner one starts the better it is. And I feel a little unhappy that not enough of this is being done by our younger anthropologists who are coming out of our University departments in all parts of the country. On the other hand, the younger generation of anthropologists are far more adventurous than we were. In terms of their theoretical interests, in terms of their topics which they take up for investigations they are far more adventurous than we were.

And the topic of the seminar which will be conducted today and tomorrow shows that they are so adventurous in taking up newer areas for investigation and relatively unexplored areas. It is an area which is relatively unexplored not only in Indian Anthropology but also in Anthropology anywhere. And I therefore congratulate you for taking up such a problem, for having the boldness and the initiative to take up such a problem and to enter into it. I wish you every success in your venture.

Thank you very much !

The Key Issue : Development, Displacement and Resettlement**

N. Subba Reddy*

All forms of development and change seem to entail some measure of displacement which in its turn calls for readjustment and resettlement. The birth of independent India itself was attended by a colossal displacement of people with the result that the Constitution of our country, in its 7th Schedule, made a provision for the resettlement of persons uprooted as a consequence of partition of the country. I happened to visit Delhi a few years after independence and stayed with an M.P. in a sprawling block of newly constructed flats. Just opposite, there were a number of tents in which refugees from Punjab were housed. There was a joke making rounds in Delhi at that time that the capital of free India was full of misplaced persons (M.Ps) and displaced persons (D. Ps).

While the Constitution of India made a provision for partition refugees, it did not provide for project refugees. It

* Senior Fellow, Centre for Economic and Social Studies, Hyderabad-500 016.

** Key-Note address delivered at the Seminar on "Developmental process and the problems of Rehabilitation and Relocation of the Uprooted" March 13-14, 1989, Madras, is indeed a glaring omission considering the penchant of the makers of new India for development projects. One can distinguish between two sets of causes for large scale displacement of people. One set of causes like natural catastrophies, wars, internecine conflicts, famines *etc.*, cannot be predicted or controlled. The other set of causes relating to different kinds of projects for the development of irrigation, power, mining, industry *etc.*, are not unforeseen occurrences and hence the extent of displacement can be visualised and provided for. The founding fathers of our nation must have thought that the Governments of the States would find a suitable solution for each problem of displacement as it arises. I would have taken that expectation to be reasonable had I not attended a symposium on involuntary resettlement of people at Zagrab in July last.

The organiser of the symposium Dr. Cernea, a Social Scientist attached to the World Bank, thoughtfully invited not only social scientists who had studied the problems of resettlement but also some administrators who were actually handling job of resettling displaced persons. One of the session drew attention to the current problems of displacement in the Narmada river project. There was an officer representing the Madhya Pradesh Government at the session. When the discussion centred round the tremendous problem of resettling thousands of people from the vast areas that would be submerged, the official treated the whole matter lightly. He said in a very casual way that many tribals who were asked to leave their forest homes were volunteering to go and settle down in cities like Bhopal. He appeared to believe that the project was a od send opportunity for those people to modernise themselves.

I am mentioning this because it shows how happy an administrator could be if he can remain immune to the realities around him and does not have to know the feeling of the poor tribals who have to leave their homes. One was tempted to ask the officer whether he would consider it an opportunity if he were to be banished from India so that he could migrate to more prosperous countries in the world where his talents might perhaps find greener pastures. We have to ask ourselves whether that officer was typical or atypical of the class of bureaucrats. In any case this example shows how one party which has to deal with another party caught in a life and death situation could have a perception which is the very opposite of that of the latter. It is here that the role of social scientist as an honest mediator comes in.

To go into the details of the Narmada project (including Narmada Sarovar Project in Madhya Pradesh and Sardar Sarovar Project in Gujarat), there is a raging controversy over the costs and benefits. The protagonists of the project claim that it will produce 2450 M.W. of electricity while the critics say that when the irrigation system is fully developed, the electricity produced will be only a quarter of that estimate. They cite the evaluation report of the late Secretary for Irrigation in Madhya Pradesh Government, Mr. Gupta, in their support. Also according to the calculation of the Ministry of Environment and Forests, the project has a long-term potential of producing only 523 M.W. of electricity. Regarding the extent of land to be irrigated again there are wide variations in the estimates. The optimists place the estimate place the estimate beyond 3,000,000 ha. (*Probe*, February 1981) while the pessimists say that it can directly irrigate only 123,000 ha. (*Times of India*, 5th October, 1988). In respect of its cost and schedule of completion, one view is that it requires Rs. 15,000 crores and 10 years to complete, while the other view is that the costs may go up by 4 times and the time taken to complete may be 30 years.

All are agreed that the project would submerge about one lakh hectares, including rich forests, and displace about 150,000 people living in 190 villages. The Department of Environment and Forest estimated that timber loss in the forests will come to about Rs. 40,000 crores. I am not good at cost-benefit analysis in material terms, and hence I leave that alone. But what is of greater importance is the question of human costs. What is going to happen to the people who will be displaced ? The most funny thing that happened was that the Ministry of Environment and Forests gave clearance for the project in April, 1987 without a thorough examination of resettlement programme and the proposed manner of its execution. Instead, it made a pious recommendation that studies should be conducted and suitable plans be evolved for resettlement. But when once clearance was given, can any further studies swerve the Governments from their chosen path?

The concerned State Governments are said to have worked out some schemes of resettlement. The Government of Gujarat is said to be prepared to fund resettlement even to the extent of Rs. 600 crores. Indeed a sportive offer is made that Gujarat will resettle displaced persons from any of the three states concerned. But the details of the sites indentified for relocation are not available. In the state of Maharashtra where the dimensions of the project and its consequences are comparatively small, it is estimated that 12,000 hectares are needed for the resettlement programme. But so far only 3,000 hectares are identified, that too in a denuded forest. It should be noted here that the State of Maharashtra is perhaps one of the most progressive among the Indian states, and they were the first to enact the Resettlement of Project Displaced persons Act in 1976. Still there is no guarantee that they would be able to resettle the displaced persons in any reasonably satisfactory manner.

The proposed National Test Range is another example of callous disregard on the part of administrators for the feelings of the people to be displaced from their ancestral homes. Governments should not visualise themselves as efficient packers and movers of human consignments. At Baliapal, in Orissa, the project of N.T.R. originally envisaged evaluation of 100,000 persons living in 130 villages. When the people organised themselves and put up stiff resistance, the Government scaled down the dimension of the project to cover 68 villages inhabited by 60,000 people. The question that comes to one's mind is why the Government originally stretched the project to cover 130 villages if it could do by displacing the inhabitants of 68 villages. It is again evidence of the same insolent nonchalance towards the cheap human commodity. First of all why locate such a project in a fertile and densely populated area ? Any sensible government should exercise all the care so as to choose a course of action which would cause the least amount of human misery even it becomes really unavoidable.

Social scientists interested in human welfare have an obligation to set out some guidelines on matters of this nature. It is not that we are opposed to all projects, but we have to plead for certain safeguards to project the interests of persons who are to be displaced by the projects, so that they would not be discarded as incidental victims of the process of development. First and foremost, the details of resettlement programme should be worked out and should be shown as the first charge on the project outlay. Apart from the physical costs, there are the human costs, and no civilised society should fail to take note of them. Secondly, the process of resettlement should be initiated early and go ahead of the project proper. While figuring out the differential human costs of resettlement, one has to keep in mind the following factors : While the initial distress due to displacement is natural to all, its long range impact differs from group to group depending on their levels of socio-economic development and the related coping capacity. Here one can broadly identify three levels, *viz.*, the tribal, the peasant and the urban.

It can be safely generalised that people of the first level (the tribal) will find the resettlement process most difficult. While those who are more advanced may have greater resource to cope with the problem. Hence I may mainly deal with the problems of resettling the uprooted tribals, not only because the difficulties of coping are greater in their case, but even in quantitative terms the number of tribes displaced by development projects happen to be much greater than other sections of the society. The Working Group on the development of Scheduled Tribes during the VII Plan period estimated that almost every development project in India invariably resulted in the displacement of tribals, and their proportions among the uprooted ranged from 52% to 100% from project to project. While I am dealing with the problem mainly from the perspective of displaced tribals, what I say applies even in the case of other small peasants, artisans and landless labourers living in rural India,

The perceived world of the tribal is much smaller than that of an urban citizen or even an average peasant. He lives in a cloistered life of his own, whether he is a subsistence cultivator, shifting cultivator, hunter or food-gatherer. A mistaken impression may exist that the latter category of people are, nomads who should not find it difficult if they are shifted to some other place. What is important to note in this context is that even bands of hunters and food-gatherers have well recognised claims to certain territory which they jealously guard and within which they live in a state of ecological balance, achieved over centuries and even millennia. It is not easy for them to eke out a living in a different kind of terrain, unless they go through a long phase of adaptation and adjustment.

Like the physical world around him, the social world of the tribal is also narrow. His kith and kin live within a narrow radius from his home. Hence he does not possess the advantage of having his relatives and friends in distant places to help him to resettle by offering him material and moral support. Hence when the tribals are to be displaced, any administrator or agency should think in terms of community resettlement and not individual resettlement. A tribal lives as an integral part of a cohesive social world which is small in dimensions. His relations and interactions with fellow humans do not partake of purposive associations as in the case of an urban citizen. He relates himself to others in what may be described as multiplex relations which implies that the same set of people figure as kins, neighbours, economic collaborators, religious participants, juridical and political councillors and defenders of their common territory. It is not easy for the tribals to forge sequestered relationships with a large number of persons in an impersonal setting. Hence it should be insisted that in any resettlement programme, a community of tribals who have known one another and can interact easily with one another should be shifted together from the old habitat to a new habitat. Being in the midst of the known social world will provide them the necessary psychological cushion and inner resource and help them to adjust to the new situation.

I have not made any intensive study of the processes and problems involved in the resettlement of displaced persons,

But my observations of a few resettlement colonies confirm the importance of the dimension of community. Like the physical infrastructure, people need a social infrastructure, without which a group disintegrates. An illustrative case is that of a colonization scheme in the Parvatipuram Taluk of Srikakulam District. With the laudable intention of weaning away the tribals from shifting cultivation the government brought down some tribal families from the interior region to a newly built colony where alternative means of livelihood in the form of settled cultivation was sought to be provided. One such colony was located at Jatapu Kotapadu. It had 100 newly built houses. 300 acres were set apart for reclamation, of which 100 acres were to be brought under irrigation from a nearby stream. Draught animals were distributed as also some seed money. But of the 100 families that were gathered there, 49 families left the colony in the first few years itself. Since then no effort on the part of the officials could stem the trend of desertions.

The main reason for the failure of the colony was that the officers in charge of it never perceived the importance of community cohesion. The recruitment of members was done in a haphazard way. In some cases, the settlers were persons who had quarrels in their families and hence chose to leave their homes. In some other cases they were persons who contracted unorthodox marriages inviting excommunication. On the whole, the members represented disparate elements assorted from different localities. They could not evolve a community life or forge a common leadership. There was no priest in the village nor a place of worship. The people had to go to their former places to conduct their rituals or to seek the help of a medicine man. The allotments of agricultural plots among different families could not proceed smoothly. There was not enough wet land to be distributed among all the families. Corporate decisions and collective actions were not possible in the kind of medley that the colony was. So it declined and disintegrated rapidly.

If there are some people, for instance like the official of the Madhya Pradesh Government, who think that this is an argument to pamper the tribals or to keep them as museum specimens instead of forcing the pace of their change, they need to look at some examples from the urban resettlement programmes in advanced countries. There too, factors like class, community, and culture have been of undeniable importance. Harrington gives some interesting instances from urban America where some of the housing projects could not become healthy residential quarters because of what he calls bureaucratically enforced rootlessness. He cites the case of a low cost housing project where at first a cohesive life had been built up, but the leaders of the community soon became disqualified to stay there because their income rose above the officially prescribed limit. The result was that the housing colony became leaderless, and the community soon developed fissures. Some housing colonies did not attract new members because of their inter-racial character. The well known British sociologist, Sprott mentions that when people reared in the 'intimacies of slums' were given flats in a housing estate in Sheffield, they found it difficult to adjust themselves to the impersonal formalities in the new environment. And when foremen and workers of a factory in Liverpool were put together in a housing estate built for them, good neighbourly relations could not develop as the latter resented the superior airs of the former even in residential quarters.

This should lead us to pay attention to the question of inter-relations between the host community and the new settlers. The displaced persons may not be always resettled in exclusive colonies or villages of their own. They may have to be settled sometimes in habitations where there are already old resident communities. Sometimes, the way of life of the immigrants may not fit into the norms and customs of the host community. D.N. Majumdar gives an example of a group of Santal families driven to live in an industrial town. A conflict arose when a Santal girl was insulted by a member of the larger community living in another part of the town. The old Santal custom had a mechanism for removal of tensions of this sort. In their tribal habitat, if a member of one village injures or insults a member of another village, the leader of the latter village sends word to the leader of the former village that their men will come on an appointed day to seek traditional reprisal. On that day they can go to the other village and beat up the offender or his relatives and break some pots and pans in their homes and return. The village at the receiving end is not supposed to resist or retaliate. Underlying this practice is the concept of collective responsibility and collective acceptance of guilt. But how can such a solution work in an urban setting where the Santals are huddled together with other communities who do not subscribe to their norms. In this particular case, when Santals in the industrial town tried to resort to their traditional mode of reprisal, they were soundly beaten up and driven back.

This may appear to be an unusual case. But it is important that any agency entrusted with resettlement work should be able to foresee possible areas of conflict between the host community and the immigrants. For instance where there is already a high man-land ratio, and the employment market is overcrowded, any further influx of people will create tensions. Other possibilities of socio-cultural conflicts should also be looked into.

The easiest and perhaps the worst way of tackling the problems of project-displaced persons is to pay them some cash compensation and drive them out into the wide open world to swell the numbers of destitutes or to join the people struggling in the unorganised sectors in urban areas. No displaced person should be taken as properly settled unless he is provided with a resource base. If the displaced persons have been cultivators of land, they should be provided with land calculated to yield them a little more income than they were enjoying before. While this looks simple, there are some difficulties in dealing with it in the context of tribal realities. The right to land of the tribal cultivator may be customary and not legal in the strict sense of the word. If administrators insist on legal interpretation of things, it would cause immense harm to the tribal. In many of the interior villages, land settlement records may not be there. Hence the tribal's customary right should be respected without insisting on legal formalities. There is a tendency to think in terms of market values and to compensate a tribal on the basis of land values in his remote habitat. In the interior tribal villages, the market values of lands may be low, but the yield may provide an assured livelihood to the cultivator. But in the plains where the density of population is more land of equivalent monetary value may not yield even a fraction of the output of the former. What is essential is that any displaced person should be able to earn better income on the resource to be provided to him in the new place. In some cases the people may not be able to produce any legal titles, but still they may be having usufructory rights to the natural resources around them like forests and water fronts. They too need to be provided with a resource base which would enable them to live a secure life. What is of crucial importance is that a person subjected to involuntary resettlement should have a say regarding the scheme of rehabilitation.

It should be noted that when people are displaced from their villages they leave behind not only their houses and lands but also some community assets like shrines, grazing grounds, forests, water resources, community halls *etc.* Hence when people are resettled care should be taken to provide them with all such common facilities, also making sure that there are schools and hospitals in their vicinity. The norms to be adopted in this regard is not that people should be helped to attain the same level and quality of life as before the time of their displacement but they should be given some extra benefit which would cover the human costs of uprootment. The stress and strain which the uprooted persons go through have been summed up succinctly by Michael Cernea, in his communication to the Anthropology Newsletter of the American Anthropological Association (Vol. 29, No. 6, Sept. 1988) : "The people affected by involuntary relocation see their livelihood taken away, their houses, lands, forests, temples and graveyards submerged, and their cultural identity threatened. The record of involuntary resettlement operations is one of the cloudiest pages in the history of induced development change". Hence to compensate for this kind of mental agony, the resettlement agencies should provide displaced persons with a more secure resource base than they have had in the old habitat.

Only the educated, the artisans and skilled workers should

be settled in towns after giving them some further training and orientation. Illiterate tribals or peasants should not be driven into the towns, and they should not be forced to become destitutes or labourers in the unorganised sector facing fierce competition from the more sophisticated sections. If it is an irrigation project, certain stretches of land in the command area should be compulsorily acquired for the resettlement of displaced persons. If a ratio of 1 : 10 is to be insisted between the area to be submerged and the area to be irrigated, at least one-tenth of the command area should be acquired for distribution among the displaced persons. The land acquisition Act with its emergency regulation should be put into use in this regard (and not for evicting people for the construction of the project). The land owners who benefit from the irrigation project should not grudge giving up a part of their land in return for future gains. The proportion of land to be acquired for this purpose of resettling the displaced in the command area may be determined in a progressive scale of land holdings of the residents of the area.

It has become a usual practice for administrators to promise that one person in each family to be displaced will be given a job on the project. Here the natural process of the domestic cycle as it obtains among the tribal society is more often ignored than not. The project work may go on for years, but what is one family at the time of its commencement may become three or four families in the course of half a decade as the nuclear family is the norm among the tribes, and sons establish separate homes as soon as they are married. The project officers may say that their list does not include the new families, and it invariably leads to hardship and heart burning. Hence all the adolescents in the affected community should be registered with the rehabilitation agency for employment at the commencement of the project.

Most important is the requirement that a detailed plan of resettlement backed by financial allocations should be built into the project outlay, and it should not be treated as a wayside contingency. The work of resettlement should be entrusted to an autonomous body and it should not be carried out by the same agency which carry out the project work.

Here one of the guidelines of the World Bank deserves to be quoted : "Longitudinal anthropological studies and past experience in many projects have shown that vesting operational responsibility for planning and executing resettlement in the agency which is specialised in, and executes, the engineering and technical works of the project, often relegates resettlement to the status of a low priority task. Therefore the guidelines recommend setting up a distinct organisational responsibility in the project, with adequate budget and staffing for implementing relocation and socio-economic re-establishment".

In the Indian context it is mostly the revenue department that is entrusted with the work of resettlement while the engineering department looks after the project work. Not even the Social Welfare or the Tribal Welfare Departments are actively associated with the resettlement process. This pattern should change and an autonomous body consisting of members of the Social Welfare and Tribal Welfare Departments, social scientists, social workers and representatives of the displaced persons should be constituted to carry out resettlement work. This body may have an officer from the revenue department as member-secretary, and all the funds earmarked for resettlement should be kept at the disposal of this autonomous body.

SECTION I

Repatriates and Resettlement

1

Exodus of Indian Minorities from Burma and Sri Lanka—A Political Background

V. Suryanarayan*

Mass movements of people—refugees, repatriates and other migrants—across national borders have increased manifold in the years since the end of the second world war. The abrupt and massive displacement of thousands of people from their land of adoption for generations causes innumerable problems of adjustment—human and political-both for the people concerned and the countries to which they migrate. The impact of these problems, which is global in character, is of special concern to India. In the post—independence period India has faced stupendous problems as a result of influx of refugees from Pakistan, Bangladesh, Tibet, Burma, Uganda and, during recent years, repatriates from Sri Lanka. The odyssey of Sri Lankan repatriates still continues with no immediate prospect to an end to their suffering.[1]

* Director, Centre for South and Southeast Asian Studies, University of Madras, Madras—600005.

In this paper, I have tried to trace the political background to the repatriation—or rather expartriation and, in some cases, even deportation—of the Indian communities from Burma and Sri Lanka. The tragic tale of these forgotten children of Mother India is a clear illustration of the failure of New Delhi to articulate and pursue a meaningful policy, towards Indian Overseas. And what is more, the agony, suffering and continuing trauma to which the Sri Lankan repatriates are subjected to show the callousness and indifference of the governments of New Delhi and Tamil Nadu.

Condemned and despised in their native villages, whether in Bengal or Madras Presidency, the Indian working classes braved the seas, provided the much needed labour to clear the swamps in lower Burma and malaria infested jungles in Ceylon and, in that process, also became the most exploited and vulnerable sections of the population. The misery, squalor and suffering to which they were subjected in the land of their adoption continues, perhaps in greater measure even after their return to the land of their forefathers as "honoured citizens" of the country. The *laissez-faire* policies of the British Raj and the ultra-nationalist policies of the independent governments have contributed to this unparalleled saga in human misery.

The greatness of a civilization, Mahatma Gandhi once said, can be judged by the treatment afforded to its minorities. The term minority has been defined by the Secretary General of the United Nations "as a group (which differs from a predominant group within a state) whose members share a common ethnic origin, language, culture or religion and are interested in preserving their existence as a national community or their particular distinguishing characteristics".[2] It is an internationally accepted axiom that a minority has the right to live in the country which has been its home for a long time. It is unfortunate that the Constitution of Burma, 1947 and the subsequent Constitutions did not confer the status of minority to the Indian community nor were built-in provisions included in the Constitution to safeguard minority rights. In the same way, neither the Republican Constitution of Sri Lanka, 1972 nor the Gaullist Constitution of 1978 gave the status of a minority to the Indian Tamils. It took nearly four decades of political turmoil and considerable loss of life and property during the four years of ethnic conflict, 1983-1987, before the Sri Lankan leaders accepted the fact in the India-Sri Lanka Accord of July 1987 that Sri Lanka is a multi-racial, multi-lingual and multi-religious country. Will the spirit of the Accord get implemented in practice ? Time alone can provide the answer to this multi-million dollar question.

It must also be mentioned that the outbursts of Burmese and Sinhalese nationalists that the Indian minorities were "flooding" into their countries ; "swamping" the indigenous people and "squeezing" them out of their own countries are not borne out by facts. In his excellent study of the Indian minority in Burma, Dr. Nalini Ranjan Chakravarti has, after analysing the various published statistics, come to the conclusion that Indian minority never exceeded three per cent of the population.[3] As far as Ceylon is concerned, the student is faced with the same dilemma. While the Sinhalese nationalists regarded the plantation Tamils as a "political, economic and social threat to the safety and well-being of the Sinhalese", the British planters were very keen to have an unfettered flow of labour from South India. In the 1920s, when the British government in India threatened to stop immigration of Indians into Ceylon, a delegation of prominent Ceylonese went to New Delhi to successfully persuade the British not to impose such a ban. When finally, the ban was imposed it was due to Indian nationalist pressure on the British government. While it may take time for the historian to deliver the final verdict, all available evidence indicates that Burma and Sri Lanka have suffered irreparable damage by evicting the Indian communities from their countries.

The immigration of Indian community in Burma is closely intertwined with the development of colonial economy. The launching of rice cultivation on a commercial scale for export and the consequent demand for cheap labour ; the export of rice which led to the development of shipping industry which required a regular supply of dockyard labour ; the development of timber mills, construction of railways and oil refineries demanding the use of extensive labour—all these led to the flow of Indian labour into Burma. The economic development was financed by Indian Chettiars, Marwaris, Multanis and

Gujaratis. The usurious Chettiars, who lent money to the peasantry, gradually strengthened their stranglehold on the economy and considerable land was alienated to these "absentee landlords". The "Chettiar colonialism" within "British colonialism" naturally fanned radical nationalist feelings among the Burmese. From the 1920s a large number of educated people also went to Burma and they became doctors, lawyers, teachers, trade unionists and also provided the large reservoir of clerical personnel. Petty trade came under the control of the Indian community. And at the lowest rung of the social ladder, there was an army of Indian sweepers, rickshaw pullers, dockyard labourers and other menial workers. Rangoon, the capital of Burma, virtually became an Indian city.

As the nationalist movement in Burma began to gather momentum, it also took an anti-Indian dimension.[4] The alienation of vast tracts of agricultural land to Indian Chettiars, the Burmese entry into the labour market following the depression of the 1930's which was hitherto an exclusive Indian domain ; the opening of the University of Rangoon and consequent turning out of Burmese graduates searching for clerical jobs—all these provided the fertiliser for the growth of anti-Indian sentiments. There were large scale riots against the Indians in Rangoon in the late 1930s. The Burmese nationalists not only wanted freedom from British political domination ; they were equally keen to throw out the yoke of Indian economic straglehold.

The period of Japanese occupation, 1942-1945, was the darkest period in the history of Indian community in Burma. The war totally destroyed the pre-war economy and the commanding position which the Indian community enjoyed. Some Chettiars had the foresight, saw the writing on the wall and even before the war began they repatriated their vast wealth from the country. But the majority of Indians suffered untold misery and hardship. Nearly 500,000 Indians left the country and out of these nearly half of them perished on the way. Those who were left behind in Rangoon joined the Indian National Army in large numbers, at a later period, they also supported the Burmese demand for independence.

The independent government of Burma introduced large number of progressive land reforms which hit the interests of the Chettiars adversely. The Standard Rent Act, Tenancy Disposal Act, Agricultural Debt Relief Act, Land Nationalisation Act, Agricultural Bank Act and Burma Foreigners Act—all these had the cumulative effect of depriving the Chettiars of their enormous wealth. No one, with a tinge of social conscience, could protest against these progressive measures. At the same time, the compensation paid was very meagre, what is more, the Chettiars found it difficult to repatriate their money into India due to stringent foreign exchange restrictions.

When the new Constitution was promulgated, it was stipulated that those who had been in continuous residence in Burma for eight out of the last ten years or for ten years immediately following the war were eligible for citizenship. But the immediate prospects were so uncertain that most Indians were reluctant to apply for citizenship. Only 400,000 applications were received for citizenship and out of these 10 000 were granted citizenship.[5] The rest were treated as aliens. When the Burmese government introduced Burmanisation of public services in the 1950s large number of Indians employed in railways, water transport, customs, post and telegraphs, public works and other departments were retrenched. In the 1960s under the Burmese ocialist Programme, the government even nationalised petty trade and this step affected the fate of thousands of Indians. What was more tragic, they were not allowed even to take their meagre savings, either in cash or gold, to India. The repatriates have complained of demonetisation of currency notes, expropriation of properties, confiscation of valuables and unimaginable humiliations. According to the recent Policy Note issued by the Tamil Nadu government, from June 1963 onwards, 1,44,353 Burmese repatriates have returned to India.[6] The position of those remaining back in Burma is not very conductive and their economic, social and political status have been declining. If the present situation is allowed to continue most of them will have no other option except to return to India.

The position of the Indian community in Sri Lanka provides a sharp contrast to that of Burma. There were not many capitalists among them, on the other hand, most of them were plantation workers. Secondly, there was not much of a nationalist movement in Ceylon before the Second World War. And consequently not much anti-Indian feeling and violence. Ceylon was politically a backwater. However, the Indian community suffered innumerable hardships including the Damocles sword of statelessness.

Like Burma, the large scale migration of Indians to Ceylon took place under the British Raj. They were taken to the island by the British colonialists to provide the much needed labour in the coffee, tea, rubber and coconut plantations. They formed the bulk of labour which turned the malaria infested forests of Sri Lankan economy even today. The agony and suffering undergone by the Indian "coolie" under the British Raj and Planter's Raj were innumerable and need not be recounted here. The verdant carpet of green in the central parts of the island, which has made Sri Lanka the veritable "island paradise" was due to the sweat and agony of Indian plantation workers. But the plantation worker was the worst victim of imperialist exploitation and, after independence, the ultra-nationalist politicians in Sri Lanka. Apply any yardstick-per capita income, living conditions, longevity of life, educational attainments, status of women—the Indian Tamils are in the worst position today.

As long as the British rule continued in Ceylon, the Indian Tamils had the same legal status as the Sinhalese and Sri Lankan Tamils, for all were British subjects. The British government insisted and allowed the emigration of Indians on the express stipulation of equality of Indians with the rest of indigenous population. But with the introduction of constitutional reforms and along with it the right of franchise, the Indian question became a live problem. Colombo wanted to absorb only a small quantum of Indians. From this they argued that it is necessary to prescribe some rigid test for proving the permanent abiding interest of the Indian community in Sri Lanka. Herein lies the seeds of the theory of "absorbable minimum" put forward by successive Ceylonese Prime Ministers since independence. Their aim was not to deny the right of franchise to the Indians, but to restrict it to the minimum. The inherent discrimination in these provisions was pointed by G.S. Bajpai as follows : "The Indian who has worked in Ceylon is to be thrown back into India as a squeezed lemon".[7]

Despite the restrictions on franchise, in the 1947 election held under the Soulbury Constitution, the Indian workers elected six representatives of the Ceylon Indian Congress, where no CIC candidates were fielded, they voted for the Marxist candidates and tilted the balance in their favour in about nine seats. The leftward swing of the plantation workers votes made the UNP leadership determined to debar the vast majority of the Indian Tamils from Ceylon's citizenship after independence. If the government could restrict the citizenship and, therefore, the franchise of Indians, a large number of Marxist candidates could be eliminated and the UNP could win the Kandyan Sinhalese seats easily.

The Ceylon Citizenship Act of 1948 and the Indian and Pakistani Residents Act of 1949 not only disfranchised the Indian Tamils, but it also made them stateless. When applications were invited, nearly 8,25,000 applied for Ceylon citizenship, which was clear evidence that the overwhelming majority of Indians wanted to permanently stay in Ceylon. But the government granted citizenship to only 1,34,168 applicants. All the others were characterised as "stateless". It must also be underlined that the provisions of the Citizenship Act were complicated and cumbersome and naturally the plantation workers were not able to produce certificates to the satisfaction of Ceylonese bureaucrats. The Indian Tamils were thus ostracised from the political mainstream of the country. Speaking on Ceylon Citizenship Act, Pieter Kauneman said in Parliament that even Dudley Senanayake could not comply with the clauses because, according to his own admission, he could not trace his father's birth certificate.[8]

From the very beginning, it was Colombo's implicit assumption that those who failed to qualify for Ceylonese citizenship were unquestionably Indian nationals and that New Delhi would regard them as such. In fact, as far as New Delhi was concerned, its policy was to discourage Indians Overseas from applying for Indian citizenship. In the protracted negotiations that took place between New Delhi and successive Ceylonese Prime Ministers—D.S. Senanayake, Dudley Senanayake, John Kotelawala and S.W.R.D. Bandarnaike—Jawaharlal Nehru emphatically maintained that except for those who voluntarily opted for Indian citizenship, the Indian immigrants in the island and their descendants were the responsibility of Sri Lanka. The era of statelessness thus continued and the problem appeared interminable.

With Lal Bahadur Shastri as the Prime Minister and C.S. Jha as the Commonwealth Secretary, New Delhi reversed its earlier principled stand and began to adopt a new approach on the question of stateless people in Sri Lanka. During this period, New Delhi was eager to come out of the "diplomatic isolation in South Asia" following the Sino-Indian conflict of 1962. The astute politician that Sirimavo Bhandarnaike was, she made the best out of the situation and clinched the issue in October 1964. The result was the Sirimavo-Shastri Pact in October 1964. According to this bilateral agreement, India agreed to confer citizenship on 5.25 lakh persons with natural increase in their numbers, over a period of fifteen years. This agreement was followed by another in 1974 as a result of which India was to receive another 75,000 persons of Indian origin within a period of two years, after those under the first agreement were repatriated. The entire process was expected to be completed by October 1981. Sri Lanka agreed, in turn, to absorb 3,00,000 persons under the first agreement and another 75,000 under the second as its nationals on the ratio of four Sri Lanka nationals for every seven repatriated to India.[9]

Some significant features of the Sirimavo-Shastri Pact must be underlined. It is the tragedy of Indio-Sri Lanka relations that this agreement, which had a bearing on the lives of thousands of people of Indian origin, was finalised by the two governments without taking into consideration the feelings and views of the plantation workers. The Ceylon Workers Congress, the most representative organisation of Indian Tamils, vehemently opposed the Sirimavo-Shastri Pact. The continuing trauma suffered by the people made the party revise its stand later and co-operate with the government in the implementation of the agreement. S. Thondaman, the President of the Ceylon Workers Congress has mentioned that the people of Indian origin were reduced to the status of "merchandise" by the two countries in the name of "good neighbourly relations". To quote Thondaman, "we are a community of human beings with soul, mind and body, with personality and cannot be apportioned between countries like beasts of burden on others' whims and fancies only to maintain good neighbourly relations. Humanity cannot be converted to merchandise in the modern age"[10]

The most damning indictment against the Sirimavo-Shastri Pact is the fact that though it lapsed on October 31, 1981 it did not fulfil its objectives. Even after the expiry of the Pact, the fate of many thousands still hung on the balance and the problem of statelessness continued until very recently. According to the statistics published by the Sri Lankan government in November 1988, the Sri Lankan government has yet to grant citizenship to 2,31,849 persons whereas the Indian commitment to grant citizenship was 84,064.

The scourge of statelessness was hanging like a Damocles' sword over the Indian Tamils for many years. The efforts of all trade unions and political groups representing the Indian Tamils, especially the Ceylon Workers Congress, was to get this thorny problem solved. The pressure tactics both within and outside the government, combined with direct actions like strikes, finally compelled the government to make major concessions. In January 1986, the Sri Lankan government passed legislation to confer citizenship to the residue of the accountable persons within eighteen months. Since bureaucratic red-tapism still continued to bog the issue, Thondaman decided to step up his campaign. In September 1988, he even threatened to resign from the cabinet and retire from public life if the problem was not solved immediately. Finally on November 9, 1988 a law was passed declaring that all persons, who have not applied for Indian citizenship will by law become Sri Lankan citizens. The era of statelessness thus came to an end marking the successful culmination of the Indian Tamil struggle for inalienable universal human rights.

According to the Policy Note issued by the Tamil Nadu Government in 1989, 1,16,000 families consisting of 4,60,000 persons (3,34,000 accountable persons of Indian origin along with the natural increase of 1,26,000 persons) have been repatriated to India. The number yet to be repatriated from Sri Lanka is 1,72,000 Indian citizens with their natural increase.[11] However, the more difficult and complex problems of integration of the Sri Lankan repatriates within the Indian Society and Sri Lankan citizens of Indian origin within the Sri Lankan national mainstream still remain.

REFERENCES

1. The part relating to Sri Lanka is a summary of the Author's eassy, "Repatriation of Indian Citizens from Sri Lanka—A Background", a Chapter in V. Suryanarayan, ed. *Rehabilitation of Sri Lankan Repatriates—A Critical Appraisal*, Centre for South and Southeast Asian Studies, University of Madras, 1986, pp. 1-21.
2. Quoted in N.R. Chakrabarti, *The Indian Minority in Burma—The Rise and Decline of an Immigrant Community*, London 1971, pp. XFII—XFIII.
3. *Ibid*, p. XIX.
4. For a good account of the role of the Indian minority in Burmese nationalism see Mahajani, *The Role of Indian Minorities in Burma and Malaya* (Bombay, 1960).
5. Uma Shankar Singh, "Indians in Burma", A Chapter in I.J. Bahadur Singh, *Indians in Southeast Asia*. New Delhi, 1912, p. 110.
6. Government of TamilNadu, *Policy Note on Miscellaneous Relief and Rehabilitation of Indians Overseas, Refugees and Evacuees* (Demand No. 43, 1989-90), p. 2.
7. Quoted in Babu Lal Gupta, *Political and Civic Status of Indian in Ceylon* Agra, 1868, p. 48.
8. Quoted in P. Devaraj, "Indian Tamils of Sri Lanka—Identity Stabilisation and Inter-Ethnic Interaction"' A chapter in *Ethnicity and Social Change in Sri Lanka* Colombo, 1984, pp. 146-65.
9. Letter from Lal Bahadur Shastri, Prime Minister of India to Sirimavo Bandarnaike, Prime Minister of Ceylon, October, 1964 and Letter from Indira Gandhi, Prime Minister of India to Sirimavo Bandarnaike, Prime Minister of Ceylon, January 27, 1974. *The Hindu*, October 31, 1964 and January 28, 1974.
10. S. Thondaman, *Presidential Address, Ceylon Workers Congress Twenty Seventh Convention* Nuwara Eliya, March 12-14, 1982.
11. *Policy note*, n. 6, p. 1.

2

Ecological Consequences of Rehabilitation Programmes in Andamans

D. Venkatesan* and V. Sudarsen*

Andaman and Nicobar Islands (Fig. 1) are covered with dense tropical forests with extensive tracks of mangrove forests. These islands form a chain of over 300 islands (33 islands are only inhabited mostly by repatriates, refugees and migrants), about 1000 kilometres east of the Indian coast, lies between 92° to 94° E. Longitude and 6° to 14° N. Latitude in the Bay of Bengal.

Andaman archipelago was famous during the British rule of India for the Penal Settlement established in 1858. The Penal Settlement was christened Port Blair, the headquarters of Andaman and Nicobar territory, in honour of Lt. Blair who had initiated the First Settlement. In the post-Independence period these islands have acquired great strategic importance and they are ecologically very important.

*Department of Anthropology, University of Madras, Madras—600 005,

An effort is made in this paper to understand India's rehabilitation policies with respect to the resettling various groups of people in Andaman and Nicobar Islands. Concurrently an attempt is also made to bring out the impact of these resettlement programmes on the ecology in general and the autochthonous groups of these islands in particular.

The population of these islands is 1,88,741 (Census, 1981) and it has over 30 linguistic groups (Table 1) with four remarkable ethnic and cultural strands. The four categories are—

(i) the aboriginal inhabitants of these islands ;
(ii) the descendents of convicts who have settled since the starting of Penal Settement ;
(iii) the rehabilitated settlers from East Pakistan (now Bangladesh), Sri Lanka, Burma and India ; and
(iv) the recent migrants from Indian mainland.

Ecological Background

Ecologically the Andaman and Nicobar Islands have been very stable for a long time with a great variety of tropical flora in the forests. Important plant species being exploited for commercial purposes are *Dipterocarpus sq.* (gurjan) *Pterocarpus dalbergidoes roxb* (padauk), *Terminalia bilata* (badam), *Cenarium suphulum kurz* (white dhoop), *Pterocymbium tinctorium* (papita), *Terminalia procers roxb* (white chuglum), *Albizia lebbock* (koka) *Diosphyres marmorata* (marble wood), *Sateraca alliptica* (chooi), *etc.* For a long time these aare plant species have not been over exploited. However, in recent years about two and a half millon cubic metres of timber has been extracted, one lakh hectares of forest cleared for human population and development and over 600 kilometres road constructed in these islands (Whitaker, 1985). The Andaman and Nicobar Island ecosystem has been seriously disrupted since these islands 'opened' for resettlement of the uprooted people and the influx of population increased.

Of the total area of the islands (8383 sq. km), 77.8 per cent was covered by lush green forest in 1961 (Census, 1961). Though the deforestation process increased in 1960s and early 1970s the Andaman and Nicobar Forest Department controls

FIG. 1

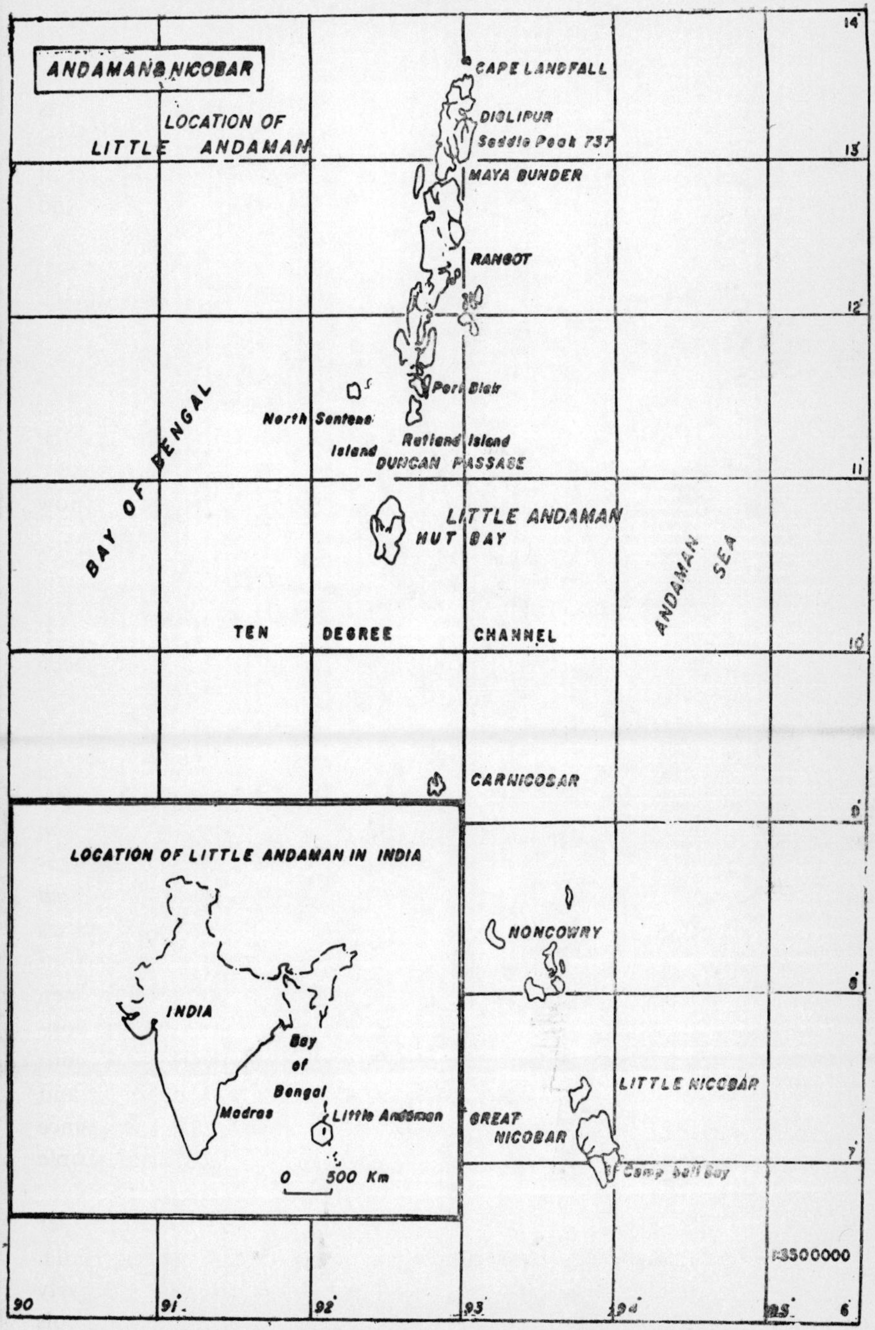
ANDAMAN & NICOBAR
LOCATION OF
LITTLE ANDAMAN
CAPE LANDFALL
DIGLIPUR
Saddle Peak 737
MAYA BUNDER
RANGOT
Port Blair
North Sentenel
Island
Rutland Island
DUNCAN PASSAGE
BAY OF BENGAL
LITTLE ANDAMAN
HUT BAY
ANDAMAN SEA
TEN DEGREE CHANNEL
CARNICOBAR
NONCOWRY
LITTLE NICOBAR
GREAT
NICOBAR
Camp bell Bay
LOCATION OF LITTLE ANDAMAN IN INDIA
INDIA
Bay
of
Bengal
Madras
Little Andaman
0 500 Km
1:3500000
14°
13°
12°
11°
10°
9°
8°
7°
6°
90
91°
92°
93°
94°
95°

TABLE 1

Ethnic groups Population based on the Language spoken in Andmann and Nicobar Islands

Language	1921	1931	1951	1961	1971
Andamanese	577	466	27	19	24
Assamese	18	8	12	13	17
Baloch	48	29	—	—	—
Bengali	1213	1171	2363	13854	28120
Bihari Ranchi	NA	NA	175	337	NA
Burmese	2490	2745	1584	1716	NA
Gujarati	206	139	125	102	159
Hindustani/Hindi	7461	11547	5074	8045	18499
Kanarese/Coorgi/Kannada	50	178	91	13	241
Karen	10	263	350	432	NA
Kharia	—	—	218	655	1166
Kiranti	283	—	—	—	—
Konkani	—	—	29	—	34
Lacadive	—	—	27	45	—
Malay	107	—	1	—	—

Malayalam	NA	NA	2815	6628	13955
Marathi	505	352	65	45	115
Munda	251	73	247	871	1065
Mundari	—	—	86	248	342
Nepali	—	—	65	165	250
Nicobari	8656	9885	11792	13930	17955
Oroan/Kurukh	83	140	1129	2212	3215
Oriya	673	191	109	127	250
Punjabi	1631	2232	224	337	1023
Phashto	464	441	15	7	NA
Sindhi/Sadri	186	83	399	1665	7
Tamil	939	769	1574	5763	14518
Telugu	385	435	1044	3756	9361
Urdu	NA	2341	862	1900	2488
Othcr Languages	266	231	191	491	2268
Asiatic Languages	364	329	28	32	13
European Languages	220	301	121	76	NA

Source : Basic Statistics 1985, Andaman and Nicobar Islands, Statistical Bureau, Port Blair.

90 per cent of land mass (Census, 1981) and at present 70 per cent of land mass is covered by forest (Whitaker, 1985). Since the islands were declared one of the Union Territories of India in 1956, experts from different fields stressed the need to conserve and manage the forests of the islands ecologically stable.

Rehabilitation Programmes

In the initial period of island development, *i.e*, between 1949 and 1961, in the fields of agriculture, public works (construction of roads and harbours), clearing the forest for cultivation and extraction of timber for commercial use demanded additional labour force. Subsequently, Government of India focused its attention on the further development of these islands. With the result, Rehabilitation Reclamation Scheme was introduced in early 1970s under the Ministry of Rehabilitation in providing resettlement to the migrants from East Pakistan (now Bangladesh), repatriates from Sri Lanka and ex-servicemen from India. Between November, 1964 and March, 1973 the Rehabilitation and Reclamation Organisation has claimed a total area of 51,400 hectares, out of which 43,818 hectares were claimed under Rehabilitation project in these islands (Govt. of India, 1975).

With the approval of Government of India each refugee and repatriate family was given 4.07 hectares of cleared forest land for agricultural purposes. Prior to the implementation of the colonization scheme in the islands, between 1949 and 1952, there were 450 East Pakistan (now Bangladesh) Bengali agricultural families resettled in South Andaman with the above land provision. Till 1961 in Andamans, there were 3,2ı7 agricultural families from different parts of India and East Pakistan resettled (Table 2), of which 2,842 families were the Bengal is (Govt. of India, 1975).

It was in the First Five Year Plan (1951-56) the maximum number (1405) of agricultural families (1,282 Bengali families) were resettled in these islands. Since Second Plan the tribals from Bihar, mostly of Chotanagpur area, were brought for labour purposes and ultimately they got resettlement provisions. There were also 64 artisan fmilies resettled in Anda-

TABLE 2

Number of refugee and repatriate families given resettlement between 1949 and 1961

Type of families	Year of resettlement	East Pakistan	Kerala	Madras	Bihar	Total
Agricultural	1949	202	—	—	—	202
families	1950	119	—	—	—	119
	1951	78	—	—	—	78
	1952	51	—	—	—	51
	1953	97	—	—	—	97
	1954	438	35	—	5	478
	1955	390	37	4	—	431
	1956	357	42	—	—	399
	1957	221	—	—	—	221
	1958	194	10	—	—	204
	1959	217	—	14	120	351
	1960	250	—	17	64	331
	1961	228	14	—	13	255
Artisan	1957	—	5	8	—	13
families	1960	12	32	—	—	44
	1961	7	—	—	—	7
Total		2861	175	43	202	3281

mans till 1961, of which there were 37 families from Kerala, 19 families belonging to East Pakistan and 8 families from Tamil Nadu. In addition, the uprooted families were also given financial assistance to supplement their economic conditions (Table 3).

The pattern of financial assistance offered to each family under the Scheme was mainly on housing, agricultural requirements, livestocks and free rations for the initial period of three years and so on. Each refugee and repatriate family and ex-servicemen family was given Rs. 6900 and Rs. 17050 respectively for the above purposes. Free rations amounting Rs. 4050 was offered to each ex-servicemen family which was not allotted to the repatriate and refugee families.

The major deforestation occurred for the settlers habitation are in South Andaman, Middle Andaman, North Andaman, Neil Island, Little Andaman, Katchal and Great Nicobar Islands (Table 4).

North and Middle Andaman

In Betapur, under Middle Andaman jurisdiction, there were 339 Bengali agricultural families who were given 820 hectares of cleared forest land for cultivation till 1973. In 1925 the British brought down thirteen Karen families from Burma to work in Forest Department as well in Saw Mill at North Andaman. Ultimately they were also given cultivable land in the forest near Mayabunder. Andaman administration brought them under land provision of local population and are settled in different areas with five acres of land per family.

South Andaman and Katchal Island

South Andaman islands including Neil Island accommodated 550 Bengali agricultural families in 1525 hectares of cleared forest land. In addition to these families in South Andaman, there were 37 Burmese families resettled to look after 202 hectares of Rubber Research Station in 1974. In Katchal, a large scale Rubber Plantation was established. Till 1974, the government cleared 520 hectares of forest and planted rubber in the proposed 2400 hectares. To look after this Rubber Plantation in the initial period there were 15 Sri

TABLE 3

Patterns of land and financial assistance given to the uprooted families in Andaman and Nicobar Islands

Type of provisions to each family	Land available per family		Money available per family	
	Rep./Refs.	Ex-ser.	Rep./Refs.	Ex-ser.
Cultivable cleared forest land	2.00 hec.	2.00 her	—	—
Homestead plot	0.13 ,,	0.40 ,,	—	—
Plantation	—	2.00 ,,	—	—
House construction	—	—	2000	5000
Agricultural tools and implements	—	—	400	—
Agricultural tools and livestock	—	—	—	3000
Seeds, fertilizers and pesticides	—	—	1500	2500
Plough animal	—	—	800	—
Livestock	—	—	800	—
Paddy bunding and soil conservation	—	—	1200	—
Wells	—	—	200	—
Households equipments and utensils	—	—	—	2500
Free rations amounting (for three years)	—	—	—	4050

TABLE 4

Refugees and Repatriates resettled in different islands of Andaman and Nicobar under the Rehabilitation Scheme up to 1975

Islands	Cleared forest already under use (ha)	Proposed forest to be used (ha)	Number of families settled	Number of families to be settled	Place of origin
South Andaman	1221 (1949-1952)	—	450 (1949-52)	—	E. Pakistan (Bengalis)
	202	—	37	—	Burma (Burmese)
Middle Andaman (Betapur)	820	—	339	—	E. Pakistan (Bengalese)
Neil Island	436	—	100	—	”
Little Andaman	390	5200	249	2200	E. Pakistan, Sri Lanka and Kerala.
Katchal	520	2400	—	15	Sri Lanka (Tamils)
Great Nicobar	844	250	100	238	India (Ex-servicemen)

Lankan Tamil repatriates settled in this island under government provisions.

Little Andaman Island

During the initial period of Rehabilitation of the uprooted in Little Andaman 249 Bengali refugee agricultural families were resettled on 390 hectares. It was in the Fifth Plan the government took more interest in bringing the island forest under resettlement programme. With the result that 5200 hectares of forest was proposed to be cleared for resettling 2200 Bengali refugees, Sri Lankan Tamil repatriates and Moplahs of Kerala. These families were planned to be engaged in agriculture since Little Andaman is flat and suitable for cultivation. Of the entire uprooted families Bengali were more in numbers. As a result at present 6406.78 hectares of forest land has been utilised for different purposes in Little Andaman (Table 5). In addition, another 20,000 hectares of forest in

TABLE 5

Forest utilization and the population composition of Little Andaman Island till 1987

Purposes of forest clearance in the island	Area covered (ha)	Number of households	Population
Hut Bay town	884.43	1755	5138
Andaman Harbour Works	121.45	—	—
Forest Plantation and Development Corporation	10.75	—	—
Reserved for Navy	246.05	—	—
Timber Industries	5.00	—	—
Harminder Bay—Nicobari Settlement	258,00	165	885
Netaji Nagar—Bengali Settlement	195.36	48	1223
Ramakrishnapuram—Bengali and Tamil Settlement	887.94	191	2446
Vivekanandapuram and Rabindra Nagar—Bengali, Tamil and Mophlah Settlement	1397.05	246	1371
Red oil palm plantation	1593.00	—	—
Forest under clearance for Red oil palm plantation	807,00	—	—
Total	6406.78	2405	11063

this island was proposed to be cleared for further human settlement in late 1970s.

Great Nicobar Island

In Great Nicobar, about 1100 hectares of forest was cleared on the west coast to resettle 338 ex-servicemen families. Initially, 100 such families were resettled under the pilot survey during 1969-70 in this island. The remaining families were resettled under the Rehabilitation Scheme till 1980. They were mostly from Punjab, Uttar Pradesh, Maharashtra, Kerala, Andhra Pradesh and Tamil Nadu. Sikhs form the second largest group while Hindu ex-servicemen being the predominant group. There are Christi an ex-servicemen too.

The Aboriginal Population

Many of the islands discussed in earlier pages have exclusively inhabited, not long ago, by the aboriginals, *viz.* the Great Andamanese, the Onge, the Jarawa, the Sentinelese, the Nicobarese and the Shompen. Their population (22,361) forms 11.85 per cent of the total population of Andaman and Nicobar Islands (Census, 1981). In Andaman District only 0.75 per cent of the tribals live in different islands because the Nicobarese being the largest group inhabited in Nicobar District. The aboriginal population (Table 6) shows a clear picture of their dwindling trend in the past few decades. Before entering into discussion on the ecological perspective of the island in terms of impact due to the developmental programmes one must understand the aboriginal subsistence ecology and their dependence on local environmental conditions.

The Great Andamanese

The Great Andamanese were earlier scattered all over the Great Andaman Islands (South, Middle and North Andaman Islands). Before the Japanese occupation of these islands the British administration resettled them in Bluff Island. In 1970, the Andaman administration again shifted them to Strait Island with an area of 3.108 square kilometres. Earlier to their resettlement in Bluff Island they were larger in numbers. The subsequent contact with 'outsiders' and developmental schemes

TABLE 6

Aboriginal Population of Andaman and Nicobar Islands

Tribal Groups	1901	1911	1921	1931	1951	1961	1971	1985*
Great Andamanese	625	455	209	90	23	19	24	28
Onge	672	631	346	250	150	129	112	100
Jarawa*	585	114	114	70	50	500	250	200
Sentinelese*		117	117	50	50	500	100	80
Shompen*	NA	NA	NA	200	NA	71	92	150
Nicobarese	NA	NA	8656	9885	11792	11902	17955	18000

*Figures of these tribes are estimated.

*Tentative population based on 1981 census publication.

have exerted great pressure on the natural resources available and led to a decrease in their population. There are only three sub-divisions among the Great Andamanese at present while they had twelve such divisions till 1920s. There is a great shift from their traditional food system (wild-boar, deer and turtle meat, fish, crabs and birds) to cereals, pulses, oilseeds, rice, wheat, sugar and so on. They have no other alternative but to adapt to these food items which are not produced by themselves. This is because of large scale destruction of forest and depletion of natural food resources in their vicinity on which they were directly dependent for their subsistence.

The Onge

The Onge were scattered all over Little Andaman Island before 1960. They were living in smaller groups and the natural resources were shared equally by all the territorial units. The area of 731 square kilometres covered with dense forest was abundant in wild-boars, edible fruits, roots and tubers. These resources were the primary food items while the marine food contributed in no less proportion to their day-to-day living.

It was during 1960s and early 1970s, under Rehabilitation Scheme, that 249 refugee families from East Pakistan were resettled on the east coast of Little Andaman clearing 390 hectares of forest. Subsequently, the Sri Lankan Tamil repatriates and the Moplah from Kerala were also given cleared forest beyond the Bengali resettlement area. In the beginning there were 28 Mophlah families and less than 50 Sri Lankan Tamil families in Little Andaman. In addition to these non-tribal population 163 Nicobari families were also brought from Car Nicobar and other Nicobar islands of Nicobar District to resettle along the east coast to establish their traditional horticultural practice on 258.75 hectares of forest during 1973. With the above conglomeration the Little Andaman population has increased to about 12,000 (Taluk Office, 1987). To develop Little Andaman economically strong the Andaman and Nicobar Forest Development and Plantation Corporation started its large-scale timber extraction scheme through private and government agencies. This cleared forest was brought under Red Oil Palm Plantation Scheme in 1973. According to this organization 1593 hectares have already been converted to Red oil palm plantations out of the proposed 2,400 hectares. Apart from these, the Andaman administration has a plan to extend the human settlement further in an area of 20,000 hectares clearing the dense forests. All these schemes requiring deforestation ultimately forced the native population of Onge to confine themselves to small pockets of the island.

As a consequence of the broad rehabilitation programmes and resultant deforestation, the Andaman administration chalked out a programme in 1976 to resettle the Onge at Dugong Creek. With the implementation of this scheme, the Onge who were enjoying the forest resources of the entire island were officially restricted to a territory of 110 square kilometres.

The competition between the settlers (Bengali, Mophlah, Tamil and Nicobari) and the natives (Onge) in Little Andaman on the available natural resources has increased since 1970s. Moreover, the settler population and the Nicobari have an advanced technique of hunting a wild-boar. Hence, the Onge face an unequal competition and hunt wild-boar and turtle by covering more area of forest and sea respectively.

The Jarawa Territory

The Jarawa have been inhabited for long time the dense forests of South and Middle Andaman following a hunting and gathering subsistonce mede. At present they are confined to 765 square kilometres of forest area along the west coast of South and Middle Andaman which has been declared as 'Jarawa Reserve'. There have been many skirmishes between the settlers and the Jarawa. Settlers like Karen, Bengali and Chotanagpur tribes living in neighbouring areas have been encroaching and exploiting the 'Jarawa Reserve' for procuring forest resources and the drifted ambergiris from the sea-shore. Andaman administration's approach to befriend the Jarawa is not quite successful, but they established contact with a local group by providing gifts like cooked food, banana fruit, coconut, cloth and so on. However, the recent attacks of Jarawa on the settlers land and houses shows unhappiness of Jarawa towards the contact with 'outsiders'. The illegal encroachment of the settlers with rifles into Jarawa territory in search of abundant natural resources and ambergiris are the major causes for human loss on both the sides in recent times. This kind of approach and exploitation will lead the Jarawa, the Great Andamanese and the Onge way.

The Sentinelese

On the other hand, the Sentinelese are isolated from the 'outside contact' inhabiting the entire North Sentinel Island. Government has been trying to befriend the Sentinelese. But the Sentinelese have been rejecting all the initiatives taken by the government and clearly shown their hostility to these attempts.

The Shompens

Shompens who live in Great Nicobar Island are a nomadic hunter and gatherer community. Their subsistence basically depends upon the forest resources. Shifting of their bands from one place to another is often found to be due to the seasonal variations in the availability of food resources in the forest. For a long time the Shompen were occupying the entire interior part of Great Nicobar with a small number of Nicobarese inhabiting the coastal regions. Traditionally the Shompen and the Nicobarese had their subsistence interdependence and shared the available natural resources.

In the post-Independence period, strategically this island became very important. After the introduction of Rehabilitation Scheme in the island in 1969 and afterwards the Shompen gradually pushed northward in search of food abundant areas. However, the competition between the non-tribals, especially the ex-servicemen, and the tribals over the available animals and plants food resources has increased in the recent years. This has led to situation of major scarcity in finding the traditional natural food for the Shompen. Though their contact with 'outsiders' is limited their dependency on environment for survival should be restored.

CONCLUSION

From the brief description of the Rehabilitation Programmes in

Andaman archipelago, it becomes quite clear how the Rehabilitation policy affects the aboriginal communities and ecology on which they depend for their survival. From this case study of Andaman and Nicobar at least two things, if not more become apparent : there cannot be a successful Rehabilitation Programme which does not take into consideration the long time effects on the already existing and inhabiting communities. The second thing is that the Rehabilitation Programmes cannot simply have as their end the settling of people in some territory. This Resettlement has much deeper connotation especially when the territory is a 'closed' one like the Islands of Andaman archipelago and the people already inhabiting are at a very low technological stage. There is no 'short-cut' method for Rehabilitation except a comprehensive one.

REFERENCES

Government of India, (1986) : *Census of India, 1981* : Andaman and Nicobar Islands, Provisional Tables.

,, (1976) : *Census of India, 1971* : Andaman and Nicobar Islands.

,, (1966) : *Census of India, 1961* : Andaman and Nicobar Islands.

,, (1928) : *Census of India, 1921* : Andaman and Nicobar Islands.

,, (1965) : *Development of special areas* : A report 1964-65. Ministry of Rehabilitation, New Delhi.

,, (1975) : Dandakaranya Development Scheme, Andaman and Nicobar Islands for Rehabilitation and Reclamation Scheme 1974-75, Ministry of Supply and Rehabilitation, New Delhi.

WHITAKER, R. (1985) : *Endangered Andamans*, World Wildlife Fund-India. New Delhi.

SECTION II

Planned Development and Rehabilitation of the Uprooted

3

Socio-Economic Problems and Social Change Among the Relocatees of Rengali Dam—A Case Study

N.K. Behura*

INTRODUCTION

Development projects sometimes require displacement of people from their traditional habitats, and voluntary or involuntary resettlement in other locations. Such relocation causes profound economic and cultural disruption to the people affected by it, and the social fabric of the communities of the area also gets disrupted. In as much as relocation involve the movement of communities from one place and environment to another, it brings about a modification of the physical and social environment in which people find themselves and to which they have to adapt after relocation. The kind and degree of physio-cultural environmental modification

The author records his gratitude for the Department of Anthropology, Utkal University, for part of the data incorporated in this paper.

*Department of Anthropology, Utkal University, Bhubaneswar.

that relocatees undergo, seems to hold a part of the clue to the total understanding of the stress, and strain they undergo ; as complete submergence of settlement, land and other immovable assets involves greater stress than partial submergence of agricultural lands. The nature of modification of the physio-cultural environment determines oustees' new demographic, economic and social circumstances. This in turn will influence the behaviour patterns which develop in the new setting, as the relocatees, having gone through the more stressful phase of relocation, respond to the new social and economic opportunities and limitations that present themselves. The nature and range of modifications brought about through resettlement seems to provide clues to an understanding of relocatees' post-resettlement behaviour and style of life. However, it has to be remembered that not all individual relocatees belonging to a single village were similarly placed either before or after relocation. Individual relocatees find the course of their life transformed in different ways.

Circumstances of the life of the people and environment of the project area change through displacement and involuntary relocation ; but these occur in conjunction with other ongoing wider processes of social change which are in operation in the area. Nevertheless, the major factors that affect the life of the oustees are their displacement and relocation.

RENGALI DAM PROJECT

Rengali Dam Project is situated in the Dhenkanal District of the State of Orissa, and has been constructed across the river Brahmani near the village Rengali of Talcher sub-division. It is situated 128 kms. north-west of Dhenkanal District Headquarters.

The original project report on the Rengali Dam was prepared in July, 1972. The construction work of the project commenced in 1973 and was completed in 1979. A masonary Dam across the river Brahmani, with a storage capacity of 4400 million cubic metres has been constructed. The project aims at controlling floods over an area of 2,600 sq. kms. in the Brahmani delta.

The Rengali Dam project is indeed a multi-purpose one, since its objectives are : (i) flood-control, (ii) generation of hydel power, and (iii) irrigation of dry land through the samal barrage constructed downstream. The command area of the irrigation scheme has been envisaged to be around 12,16,000 acres. At the moment 110 megawatts of electricity is being propagated through two units, and there is a proposal to install three more units.

Number of villages under Submergence

The reservoir of the Dam has been spread over 414 sq. kms affecting 265 villages, out of which 71 are in the Pallahara sub-division of the Dhenkanal district and 194 are in the Deogarh sub-division of the Sambalpur district. The affected villages have been categorised into the following six types :

(i)	Fully submerged villages	41
(ii)	Fully submerged villages with partly submerged agricultural lands	54
(iii)	Both village and land have been partly submerged	20
(iv)	Villages in which only agricultural lands have been partly submerged	84
(v)	Uninhabited villages that are fully submerged	31
(vi)	Uninhabited villages that are partly submerged	35
	Total number of affected villages	265

All total 9.585 families, in both the districts of Sambalpur and Dhenkanal, have been affected in a big way.

Land under Submergence

Construction of Rengali Dam affected village settlements, productive lands, people and several public institutions, which have been listed hereunder :

A. AREA OF SUBMERGENCE

(i)	Private Land	25,153 acres
(ii)	Government Land	78,729 acres
(iii)	Reserve Forest	2,023 acres
	Total area of submergence	1,05,905 acres.

B. IMPORTANT PUBLIC INSTITUTIONS SUBMERGED

(i)	High School	06 numbers
(ii)	M.E. School	20 numbers
(iii)	Primary School	88 numbers
(iv)	Public Health Centre	02 numbers
(v)	Public recognized shrines and temples	11 numbers
(vi)	Police Station	01 number

REHABILITATION POLICY

The rehabilitation of the oustees, who were numerous and most of whom were below the poverty line, and were depending upon rainfed agriculture, was a stupendous task. Payment of only cash compensation to the oustees was considered to be inadequate and unsatisfactory. Land was considered as a major humanitarian issue in resettlement and efforts were made to provide land to as many oustees as possible in order to enable them to pursue their agrarian life.

Therefore most of the oustees were rehabilitated in groups of households in nearby vacant government land in their home districts so that they would feel at home, and due weightage was given to their option in the selection of sites for rehabilitation. Land has been made available to the oustees for house sites and for the practice of agriculture.

Infrastructure facilities, such as, wells, tube-wells and tanks for water, approach roads, community or club houses, schools, shrines *etc.* were provided in each new resettlement village so that the oustees could make a beginning for rebuilding a decent village life.

Rehabilitation facilities were provided to the oustees in a sympathetic perspective, and a person who was a major and married by December 1973 was considered as constituting a separate family. And even oustees were paid compensation for the government land they had encroached.

Each family was provided with one house site of 50 decimal, and either three acres of irrigated land or six acres of unirrigated land for agricultural purposes in the resettlement villages. This land was given to all the oustees free of cost.

The oustees paid money to the Rehabilitation Agency of the Government for the reclamation of the forest land, which had been allotted to them, at the rate of Rs. 300/- per acre. But the landless displaced persons were exempted from payment of such charges, because they had not received compensation for agricultural land.

The oustees were provided with free transportation facilities for their movable assets from the submerged village to the new settlement.

Compensation was paid to the oustees for such immovable property as agricultural land of various types, house sites, houses, wells, tanks, trees, ponds *etc.*, as per rules, rates and procedures fixed up by the State Government. However, the oustees were sentimentally opposed to their displacement. The oustees had to leave their ancestral home under severe psychological stress. And officials confirm that shifting was a pathetic scene.

The evacuation work started (June 1980) after the disbursement of compensation money although new sites had already been located for their rehabilitation earlier. The oustees of a village were asked to choose a particular re-settlement village which they considered suitable from their view-point. This means that the submersible villagers had been given limited options about the resettlement site. After the selection of the resettlement site actual displacement activities started. In the first phase, the homestead land was demarcated so as to enable the oustees to construct their new houses in the resettlement village so that they could directly move to their new houses. Timber and bamboo required for constructing about two rooms were provided to the oustees by the Forest

Corporation of Orissa at concessional rate. The oustees built their respective houses in the resettlement villages at their own cost.

Rehabilitation

The villagers were expected to shift soon after they received compensation, but they waited upto the last moment, that is, only when they came to know that their houses were going to be submerged under the reservoir, they moved out from their ancestral homes (June 1983).

During the course of their movement to the resettlement villages they were provided with medical facility by a mobile medical party, and they were also given free food during their journey by the project authorities.

Their plight and tribulation indeed started in their resettlement villages. Much of their cattle got emaciated and in course of time perished for lack of grass, foliage and other kinds of fodder. They could not bring all the hay and straw from their old villages due to the lack of adequate transport facility. They themselves gradually and steadily started spending their compensation money on food, treatment, marriage and such other ceremonies. In these two study villages, which are located in the Malaygiri Reserve Forest area, oustees depended entirely on their compensation money for maintenance as the agricultural land which had been allotted to them was uncultivable.

Rehabilitation

So far 2982 families from the submerged areas have been resettled in sixty-one new villages. Out of these, twenty-five villages have been set up in the Gohira Ayacut and seven villages in Samokoi Ayacut area ; and the rest twenty-one villages have been set-up in the Reserve Forest area on Brahmani Right and eight in the Reserve Forest area on Brahmani Left. Homestead land and agricultural land have been provided to the resettlers in these villages according to resettlement norms. Infrastructure facilities such as wells, tubewells, tanks, community houses, schools, shrines, approach roads, weekly market, *etc.*, have been provided in each new village.

A total of 4,143 families from the submersible area have opted for resettlement to 95 individual resettlement clusters and 652 other locations in existing revenue villages according to their individual suitability. Accordingly ninety-five individual resettlement clusters, sixty-eight on Brahmani Right, and twenty-seven on Brahmani Left have been established with necessary basic facilities such as wells, tube-wells, tanks, schools, community houses, approach roads, shrines, weekly markets, *etc.* Thus 7,125 families have been settled by allotment of land and 2,460 have been settled by payment of cash.

The project authorities have constructed 104 ponds, 205 wells, 151 tube-wells, 85 primary schools, 30 Higher primary schools, six High schools, 69 Community Houses, shrines for each village, approach roads, shops, Health Centres, Post Offices and Weekly Markets.

Compensation

The land required for the construction of the Dam project belonged to individual owners as well as to the owners on payment of compensation. Lands were valued on the basis of the prevailing market rate of that date on which the notification for acquisition had been issued. The Government, however, paid fifteen per cent more than the estimated value to the people as their lands and other immovable assets were acquired compulsively. Nevertheless, people were aggrieved over the delayed payment of compensation to them for their submersible immovable properties. The oustees were also sore over another factor that influenced the valuation of their landed properties. For instance, for determination of land value authorities took into consideration the sale value of land in that area as ascertained from registered sale-deeds. The evacuees alleged that valuation of their lands for acquisition on the basis of registered sale-deeds was not justified because buyers often entered a lower amount in the registered sale-deeds with a view to avoiding payment of full stamp duty.

Agricultural lands in the submersible villages were classified into seven categories, for payment of compensation, taking into consideration such factors as geographical situation, quality and level of land, productive capacity, moisture retention capacity, *etc.* Homestead land was kept as a separate category. The rate per acre of land was as follows :

Sl. No.	Type of land	Compensation per acre (Rs.)
1	2	3
1.	Bahal or low paddy land	4,500
2.	Berana or medium paddy land	3,800
3.	Mala or upland for paddy	3,300
4.	Goda Aula or upland for rabi crops (Category-1)	2,500
5.	Goda Sayam or upland for rabi crops (Category-2)	2,000
6.	Goda sayam or upland for rabi crops (Category-3)	1,500
7.	Patia or fallow (waste land)	500
8.	Homestead land	4,500

Compensation for houses in the submersible villages was paid to individual owners. For the purpose of assessment all the houses were classified into twelve categories on the basis of materials used, the quality of construction and the present condition. The rate of compensation varied from Rs. 190.91 to Rs. 24.78 per sq. mtr. of the plinth area, and the people did not have much to complain about it.

For payment of compensation wells were classified into four types, and the payment varied from Rs. 176.78 to Rs. 5.42 per sq. mtr. The evacuees were not happy with this rate. They alleged that it was too low. They solicited that the calculation be made as per cubic metre, but this was not accepted. Similarly, compensation for tanks and ponds was paid to the owners at the rate of Rs. 322.80 per sq. mtr. and the evacuees were unhappy about it.

Compensation for perennial fruit-bearing trees, such as, mango, jack fruit, tamarind, coconut, orange, bassia, latifolia, *etc.*, was paid on the basis of the girth of the trunk of trees. If the girth was less than one foot compensation was Rs. 5.00

and if it was above six feet the rate was Rs. 100.00 per tree. The oustees were very unhappy with this sort of calculation, because for some a fruit-bearing tree was not one of economic value but also involved emotional attachment.

Compensation for other semi-permanent fruit-bearing trees, namely, custard apple, guava, cherry, lemon, wood-apple, elephant apple, papaya, plum, berry, *etc.*, was paid on the basis of annual fruit value of a tree which varied from Rs. 1.00 to Rs. 60.00 per tree. Compensation for non-fruit-bearing classified trees, with timber value, such as *sal* (shorea robusta), *kusum* (carthamus, tinotorius), teak (tectona grandis) rose wood (dalfergia latifolia), *asan*, *bandhan*, *piasal*, *etc.*, was also paid on the basis of a girth of a tree. The rate for a tree of timber value having more than six feet girth was Rs. 180.00 and one having less than one foot girth was Rs. 9.00. The compensation for a bamboo plant varied from Rs. 1.00 to Rs. 10.00 only, which was not justifiable.

No compensation was paid for common village properties, such as school building, club house, comon house, shrine, temple, tank, well, *etc.*, because project authorities provided these infrastructure facilities in the resettlement villages.

Land for all the displaced families could not be found, and thus 2,460 families were paid Rs. 14,040/- per family in lieu of six acres of unirrigated or three acres of irrigated land and 0.5 acres of homestead land. However, so far 18,850 acres of reclaimed land has been distributed among the oustees, in addition to available fallow land.

An amount of Rs. 13,88,41,536/- which is about ten per cent of the project cost (excluding the power house) has been spent on relocation work of 9585 families. Thus the cost of relocation per family has come to Rs. 14,485/-.

In this paper social change among the relocatees of two villages which have been studied is being discussed. Both the villages are located in the Dhenkanal district.

Study Village: Khemla

Khemla, the resettlement village established in Charigachhia reserve forest area on the left side of Brahmani river has been studied. The name of the submerged village from where most of the resettlers of this new village have come was also

Khemla. The village was submerged in the monsoon season of 1982, and the people moved to the new village during the summer of the same year.

In the old Khemla village, which was situated at a distance of 2 kms from the present Rengali Dam, there were 260 families belonging to ten Hindu castes, four scheduled castes and two tribal communities. Out of the 260 families 146 have been settled in this new village and the rest 114 families have been settled elsewhere as per their own options. Out of the 114 families 93 have been settled in the Samakoi colony near Samakoi Ayacut and the rest 21 families have been settled in the reserve forest area of Rengali Left Rehabilitation Division.

The caste-wise break-up of the families in the new village is as follows :

Name of the caste/ tribal community		Number of families	Traditional Occupation
	(Hindu Caste)		
1. Chasa	,,	47 families	Farming
2. Gauda	,,	5 ,,	Dairy farming and water supply
3. Gudia	,,	3 ,,	Confectionary
4. Kumbhar	,,	5 ,,	Pottery
5. Teli	,,	4 ,,	Oil extraction
6. Thoria	,,	22 ,,	Small itinerant trading
7. Bhandari	,,	5 ,,	Hair-cutting and ritual service
8. Kamar	,,	2 ,,	Blacksmithy
9. Keuta	,,	1 ,,	Fishing trade
10. Sundhi	,,	2 ,,	Distillation of liquor
11. Kandara-Harijan	,,	6 ,,	Agricultural labour
12. Dhoba	,,	6 ,,	Washing of dirty and impure clothes
13. Pana	,,	6 ,,	Drumming, basket-making and agricultural labour
14. Hadi	,,	2 ,,	Scavenging and Sweeping
15. Kandha Tribe	,,	5 ,,	Unspecific
16. Sahar	,,	25 ,,	-do-
TOTAL		146 ,,	

Study Village : Banara

Banara is situated by the left side of the National Highway No. 23 at a distance of one km. from Khamla. It is about 12 kms from Pallahara sub-divisional headquarters. In this village there are six caste groups and one tribal community. Members of the Chasa caste also outnumber all other categories. The residents of this resettlement village had come from a submerged village near the Rengali Dam, called Banara. All the residents of the old village have moved to this new village *en bloc.*

The caste-wise break-up of the families in Banara village is as follows :

Name of the caste/ tribal community		Number of families		Traditional Occupation
1. Chasa	(Hindu Caste)	31	families	Farming
2. Gauda	,,	9	,,	Dairy farming and water supply
3. Gudia	,,	1	,,	Confectionary
4. Teli	,,	2	,,	Oil extraction
5. Thoria	,,	10	,,	Small itinerant trading
6. Dhoba	Harijan	4	,,	Washing of dirty and impure clothes
7. Kandha	Tribe	17	,,	Unspecific.
TOTAL		74	,,	

The oustees are confronted with innumerable problems in their relocation settlements, and instead of being treated with sympathy they are treated with disdain and derision by the people of the area who have not been affected by the construction of the Dam. The oustees are referred to as *budi loka* (submerged destitutes) and *bastuhara* (people deprived of their hearth and home). Thus in the estimate of the unaffected people of the area the oustees occupy an inferior social position.

SOCIO-ECONOMIC PROBLEMS

Problems of Land

Land is very important for the oustees as agriculture is the back-bone of their economy. In this resettlement village of Khemla each family has been allotted six acres of land for agricultural purposes without any consideration of one's land holding status in the old village. The relocatees, particularly the members of the Chasa caste, who possessed land in the old village, are not happy with the policy of equal distribution of land in the resettlement village. They contend that this has been done without paying due attention to the agricultural background as well as to the family size among the relocatees. Moreover, those oustees who had large land holdings in the old village had a place of distinction in the village socio-economic structure. They were being respected by small land-holders and the landless, because in the rural agrarian social structure land determines the social position of a person. Substantial farmers used to employ the landless as wage-labour and used to help the needy. Therefore, the large landholders and substantial farmers were being held in high esteem by others in the old village. In the resettlement village they have been reduced to the level of other relocatees, and this phenomenon has caused a lot of resentment among the erstwhile substantial farmers. In the old village the members of the Chasa caste possessed 348.97 acres of agricultural land out of a total of 649.24 acres. Though household-wise they constituted 30.17 per cent, they possessed 53.75 per cent of land in the village. This means that they possessed more land than others. But in the new village with the allotment of six acres of unirrigated land to each relocatee family, all of them have been reduced to the same level in terms of land holding.

The other problem relating to land is that there has been discrimination in the allotment of land with regard to its quality. Agricultural land that has been allotted to the relocatees in these villages is not of one variety, but of three types, *viz. aaul*, *daima* and *saima*. *Aaul* is the best variety amongst the available land types, *daima* comes next and *saima* is the third variety. All the three available varieties of land were to be distributed equally among the relocatees. Thus the pattern of land allotment has been unequal. The relocatees belonging to the weaker section have been deprived of their shares of the *aaul* variety of land, and therefore there is discontentment amongst them. This has hampered village solidarity and harmonious community life.

The third problem that relates to land is the quality of land that has been allotted to the relocatees. They have been provided with six acres of unirrigated, undulating and stumpy land in the Malayagiri Reserve Forest area. This land has simply been reclaimed by the Project Authorities and has not been made arable. The area is rainfed, and the water retaining capacity of the land is very low because water flows down fast and torrentially causing erosion of the subsoil. In most cases the land is replete with gravels and laterites.

The relocatees were promised that all their lands would be ploughed with the help of tractors for the first time, so that it would not be difficult for them to till the land with country made plough subsequently. But the project Authorities only used tractors here and there, and as a result most of the allotted lands have remained unploughed.

From this it is evident that the resettlement policy and operation are not reassuring, because the Project Authorities through their action-plans, have failed to dispel the apprehension of the oustees, who are now totally despondent and lack self-confidence.

Problems of Employment

In the old Khemla village, all the residents had either a direct or indirect stake in agriculture. There were large land-holders who could engage the landless in their agricultural operation on payment of wages. There were casual as well as contractual labourers. The land-holders in the old village could absorb the unemployed people of the village to a significant extent.

In the resettlement, every family has been allotted six acres of unirrigated, infertile and uncultivable land. However, on an average each household has managed to bring under cultivation 2.75 acres of land. The yield from these lands is very low, and therefore, there is a general deficit in every household. Notwithstanding the shortcoming in agriculture eight families are in a position to engage hired labour and 21 others are forced to engage hired labour because of lack of manpower. Whereas seven Chasa families in this resettlement village are confronted with an awkward situation. In the old village they were quite well-to-do and were regular employers of hired labour. In the resettlement village they have become almost destitutes because of their shortsighted indulgence in conspicuous consumption. Though they find themselves in constant want now, they feel it embarrassing to work as wage-labour within the village, and therefore they prefer wage-earning outside their village.

The scope of wage-earning opportunity within the village as well as in the neighbouring villages is inadequate as against the demand. Greater demand for and less scope for wage-earning opportunity within the village has forced the villagers to go outside the village in search of wage-earning. Seventeen persons have left the village and have gone to distant places for earning a meagre living. Some persons during the lean agricultural season regularly go to Rengali to work as coolie, but they return home during the peak period of agricultural operation.

Fishing and Fish Trade

Due to poverty and lack of better income generating avenues 20 resettled families have taken to fishing and fish trade. Among these, there is only one family whose traditional occupation was fishing, and the traditional occupations of the rest were farming, trade and commerce, blacksmithy, pottery and washing of dirty and impure clothes. Circumstances of displacement have forced them to take to this sort of economic pursuit, which they would not have taken up in their old village because for the Chasa caste fish-trade is a lowly and degrading occupation.

SOCIAL CHANGE

Sibling Relationship

In the traditional village set-up the relationship between brothers was intimate and cooperative. Brothers always constituted a strong corporate group since their relationship revolved round ancestral land and other common assets. Occasional discords and dissensions among them were being absorbed within the system of co-residence and joint living. Each brother individually used to pay a high premium in terms of hard labour and unflinching loyalty to the family.

Normally brothers did not wish to separate nor sons intended to separate themselves from old parents. But the circumstances of displacement forced them to get separated for 0.5 acres of homestead land and six acres of agricultural land provided by the Project Authorities to all those who were married by December 1973. In some cases brothers managed to get contiguous homestead plots in the new village, and in fact lived together for some time, but they could not live together for long, and after a year or so they got separated from each other. There was no common property to keep them together. Self-interest and bickerings between spouses weakened sibling solidarity and the relationship between parent and married sons. In the new village the resettlers are trying to maximise their selfish ends within the scarce resources. Some resettlers have become so self-centred and individualistic that they even refuse to observe mortuary rites collectively with all other brothers.

Neighbours do cooperate with each other in a variety of ways, and such cooperation is invariably based on mutual benefit. All parties in a transaction or interaction meticulously strive to safeguard their respective interests. None is prepared to sacrifice his interest even a whit. This was not the case in the old village. There cooperation was spontaneous, because of the feeling of fraternity and village unity. The sense of fraternity and village unity has disappeared from the relocatees in the new village because of a grim economic situation that confronts them. The new village has been affected by stark economic problems. The adverse post-relocation situation was beyond the imagination of the relocatees. Their unmitigated economic condition is the outcome of their being agriculturally very much worse off than before, *i.e.* before displacement.

Nature of Cooperation

Cooperation is a joint or collaborative effort directed

towards some specific goal, in which common interest or hope of a regard is involved. It may be voluntary or involuntary, direct or indirect, formal or informal, but the effort is always towards a specific end, in which all the participants have a stake – real or imaginary. In human societies cooperation is an ethical norm and as a social process it is proposed up by appropriate institutional mechanism.

In the traditional village set-up relationship between members of an extended family, kin groups, neighbours fellow castemen and co-villagers was intimate, reciprocal, obligatory and cooperative, since the relationship revolved round common property, common interest and common resources. And further that relationship was not individual interest-centric rather oriented towards common welfare. That social structure was capable of nullifying occasional discords and dissensious whenever it cropped up, and it was capable of restoring normalcy. Whereas, the social structure of the relocatees in the resettlement village has developed a new trend of alienation and anomie. Being dispossessed and deprived of their age-old natural environment, the peasant resettlers have no alternative than to reconcile with the new setltement site which is located in the interior of a forest and hilly environment. They realise that they have to put up with the predicament of the new habitat, since a majority of their elders had selected this village site, and now they cannot shift elsewhere.

Causes of conflict

In the old village all the immovable properties were in the name of the household heads, who received the compensation money for their submerged property. Conflict arose in the resettlement village between father and elderly married sons and between brothers with regard to the distribution of compensation money. On receipt of this money several oustee families quickly performed marriage of their sons and daughters which had been postponed for lack of funds. And, therefore, many oustee families spent bulk of their compensation money in meeting their pressing expenses. And the balance had been kept in the custody of the household head. After displacement, sons who were married by December 1973, and as such have received homestead and agricultural land from the Project Authorities, and are now living independently demand their due share of the compensation money from their respective father's elder brothers. In some cases former household heads have paid nominal amounts to the claimants and not full shares of the compensation money under the pretext that the latter have received homestead and agricultural lands independently, and therefore this money should be shared by those sons who have not got this privilege.

In the old village, Chasa was the dominant caste group and its members virtually used to rule the village because of their intra-caste solidarity and better economic position. But in the new village their solidarity has been impaired because of intra-caste schisms and conflicts. There are several factors which have given rise to conflicts, and of these the two important ones are : (i) pursuit of socially degraded occupations, and (ii) establishment of marriage relationship with people of inferior social status.

In the new village some Chasa families, under severe economic strain, have taken to fish-trade which is incompatible with their caste position in the traditional social order. For them it is a demeaning avocation from the point of view of caste norms.

Likewise, conflict within two important lineages of the Chasa residents in the new village has also weakened their caste solidarity. Three Chasa families of the village have forged marriage relationship with Chasas of inferior category. These families accepted marriage proposals from inferior Chasas residing in other villages in spite of opposition from their respective lineage members. They did so because their own prestige has been tarnished and lowered by displacement and the stability of their economy has been shattered. Now the oustee occupy a despicable position in the entire district, and they are designated as *budi loka* or submerged destitutes. Therefore, those oustees who have preferred marriages relationship with people of inferior status are firm and non-repentant about their action. They are of the view that when the question of survival is at stake everything else is unimportant.

In the new village inter-caste conflict has also gathered sufficient momentum. In this village Chasas have lost their traditional hold over the village. Members of other castes do not pay any heed to the Chasas and they consider the latter as their equals. They have primarily developed this attitude because of the fact that all the oustee families have been allotted equal amount of land. Harijans no longer behave as 'untouchables' in the resettlement village. There is a continuous conflict raging between Harijan resettlers and caste Hindu resettlers in the village over the use of common wells, tube-wells and tanks. In the old village Harijans lived in the periphery and maintained a very subordinate position and kept a low profile with regard to the caste Hindus. In the resettlement village they do not hesitate to behave as their equals because they too have been allotted similar amount of land as others, and they have been provided with homestead land in the proximity of caste Hindu homes. Therefore, they freely use public wells, tube-wells and tanks of the village which have been provided by the project. This sort of behaviour of the Harijans is not appreciated by the caste Hindu resettlers, and therefore there are inter-caste rivalries and conflicts. The new village is not free from tensions of this sort, which disrupt the village unity.

Changing frontiers of kinship

Kinship relationships are receiving new challenges among the relocatees Kinship relationships in any society are central to its social structure. Patterned interactions, claims, obligations and sentiments are determined in a society by kinship relationships.

Kinship has to do with relationships of consanguinity and affinity. All societies distinguish various categories of consanguineal kins and affines, and associated patterns of rights and obligations. In simple societies every individual is related by kinship or affinity to everyone else and in complex societies a person's consanguines and affines are limited for practical purposes to a selected few.

Kinship systems operate on responses to various recognizable pressures within a framework of ecological, biological, psychological and social limitations. Therefore, no society can do away with kinship relations, they may only vary in the degree of intensity.

For illustration of the changing frontiers of kinship the Chasa caste among the relocatees has been selected. Marriage institution among the oustees, who are referred to as "*budi loka*" or submerged destitutes, has swifty undergone several changes. While living in the old village the Chasa were very particular about forging marriage relationship with people of similar status within the caste. The marriage field was very wide and diffused, and one could select a family for establishing fresh marital relationship out of a wide range of choice. After displacement their marriage field remained confined mostly to their fellow castemen among the relocatees as well as to those Chasa who were earlier inferior to them socially. Non-oustees are not prepared to give their girls in marriage to the relocatee families, because they apprehend that their girls would not get enough food and clothing and in all probability would be pushed to a life of misery. On the other hand non-oustees are not prepared to take brides from the oustees because they think that the former would not be able to pay ostentatious presentations of gifts, and consequently the groom's family would be looked down by their kins.

In the old village guardians of a prospective groom used to search for a suitable bride, but among the relocatees the trend is just the reverse. Now the onus lies on the bride's family, because girls are getting over-aged and with the passage of time it would be still more difficult to find suitable matches for them.

Among the relocatees lineage unity has become weak and it no longer functions as a solid social block. After displacement spatial gap, poverty and lack of social control have together contributed to the weakening of the structure of lineages. No longer members of a lineage are in a position to strictly observe pollution arising out of birth and death. Sometimes lineage members residing elsewhere are informed late about the incidence of birth and death, and consequently they do not observe the pollution thereof. This is often interpreted as a deliberate negligence.

In weddings too those members of a maximal lineage who

reside elsewhere, are not invited. There is a general lack of interest in the common observance of rituals and ceremonies among the constituent members of a lineage, because some members wilfully refrain from paying their own shares.

On wedding and other ceremonies only very close affines are invited and all those who are invited also do not participate in person, because payment of tradition-bound presentations is an insurmountable problem for them. They simply send some nominal presentations. Mobilization of kinship ties in *rites de passage* for social, economic and moral support has become a secondary action, as members of a lineage, which is a corporate group, remain indifferent to kinship obligations.

Kinship ties which provide a measure of stability to social relations are in a flux among the relocatees.

Lessons from Rengali Resettlement

The resettlement project has failed to restore, let alone improve, the social and economic well-being of the displaced population. Affected populations though had been consulted as regards the selection of relocation sites, their participation had not been ensured in the entire resettlement process. However, dissemination of information about the impending relocation, rates and procedure of payment of compensation, and about available choices of relocation sites had been undertaken among the oustees.

The oustees had put up stiff resistance against their displacement in an organized way. Therefore, the Project Authorities did not ascertain the reactions and the responses of the host populations to the proposal of resettling some displaced families in the vacant lands of their villages. Now conflicts between the resettlers and their host populations have arisen in several individual clusters, because the latter consider the former as encroachers on their limited resources. And in cluster villages population density has suddenly increased to levels above the carrying capacity of the land and natural resources available to hosts and incomers.

Here the resettlement operations though have not been left out of the main project design, it seems that adequate attention has not been paid to socio-cultural dimensions of the problem of displacement. No social survey had been conducted either among the oustees or among the host area populations in order to facilitate relocation. Before displacement, detailed resettlement plans should have been prepared on the basis of socio-economic data, so that oustees could have been spared from the post-relocation hardships.

Some implicit implications of pure bureaucratic approach, which is a feature of Rengali resettlement process, may be highlighted here. For instance, the leaders of the old Khemla village were shown several sites for resettlement within the Malayagiri Reserve Forest in the catchment area of the dam. During the time of inspection the forest was dense, cool and verdant, and the soil appeared to be swampy and fertile to the representatives of the Khemla village. The leaders identified a patch which was reclaimed and where the new village has been located. After reclamation the soil looked completely transformed. During the last ten years the sub-soil has been washed away to a large measure and the soil has lost its moisture retaining capacity. The soil is in fact sandy-loam, replete with gravels and boulders. The soil is not suitable for agriculture because it dries up immediately after the showers. Khemla and several other villages have been located in the catchment area of the dam, and the whole area is rainfed, and is beyond the purview of irrigation. A majority of the oustees have been relocated here under the pretext that no land is available in the command area of the dam. Peasants have been relocated in an area which is not favourable for good farming, hence the hardship.

In the resettlement village the traditionally non-farming castes have been allotted equal amount of land as the farming castes family-wise. Farming castes are making strenuous efforts to make their respective lands cultivable ; whereas Harijan and some other non-farming castes are not making such efforts to make their lands cultivable, as they lack resources, skill and zeal. Some Harijan resettler families have already disposed of portions of their homestead land. Agricultural land has not yet come to the market because there are no potential or real buyers within the village or in the neighbourhood. Outside buyers do not purchase these lands as these are infertile and uncultivable.

The backbone of the resettlement plan anywhere should be a 'development package', that is, a set of provisions aimed at reconstructing the production base of the relocatees. This package must offer suitable opportunities and resources for their economic and social re-establishment as self-sustaining producers. In Indian context both 'land-based' and 'non land-based' strategies need be pursued as there are farming and non-farming castes among the oustee.

In Khemla the non-farming caste groups should have been provided with adequate facilities to pursue their respective avocations, or alternatively there should have been sustained effort through extension services to generate an urge in them to undertake agriculture for self-sustenance. In this case there is no strategy at all. Excepting the reclamation work the Project Authorities/State Government have done nothing. There is no irrigation whatsoever, no agricultural extension service, no tree-crop development scheme, no commercial forestry scheme, no vocational training scheme, no off-farm employment scheme and no income-generative activities in operation in this area.

Only land-based resettlement cannot prevent major disruption in the life of the relocatees. Land is a crucial factor in the resettlement strategy. However, restoration of the productive potential of the relocatees is more important than mere provision of land. In Rengali land could not be provided to all the oustees. The pity is that lots of farming families have been deprived of agricultural land. It is a serious constraint. But the Project Authorities should have conducted a survey to find out as to who among the oustees wanted to be settled by cash compensation only. This would have been a better procedure.

In case of non land-based resettlement strategies schemes should have been developed to restore the productive systems of the relocatees by providing suitable substitutions for the lost income-generating assets, but this effort has not been made.

Environment preservation

The resettlement plan should be drawn with a specific orientation towards preserving and improving the existing environments. In Rengali, resettlement of most of the oustees has been undertaken in the upper catchment belt of the reservoir reclaiming dense virgin forests. Destruction of this forest tract has caused and will continue to cause immense harm to the life and economy of the inhabitants of the area. The denuded environment has been aggravating the post-displacement miseries of the oustees.

4

The Tiger Triumph and the Timid Tribal : The Chenchu Case

V. Gangadhar* and D Padmavathi**

The dwindling number and disappearance of some of the most valuable species and wild-life are attributed mostly to, (1) indiscriminate cutting down of forests, (2) dereserving areas for developmental activities, and (3) indiscriminate poaching. To preserve wild-life, a comprehensive wild-life (protection) Act was enacted in 1972. Special conservation projects for endangered species like hungall (1970), lion (1972), tiger (1973), crocodile (1974) and brown antler deer (1981) are implemented.

A million dollars from the World Wild Life Fund was earmarked for the tiger project launched on April 1, 1973. The aim was to develop natural forest environment free from human interference, so that the tiger population increases ; it

* Dept. of Social Anthropology, S.V. University, Tirupati—517 502.

**Centre for Women Development Studies, Mahila University, Tirupati—517 502.

was named Project Tiger. The Government of India extended the Project Tiger scheme to Andhra Pradesh during 1982-83. Srisailam-Nagarjun Sagar Sanctuary with an area of 3568.00 sq. km was chosen for the implementation of Project Tiger. This tiger reserve is located in the districts of Mahbubnagar, Kurnool, Prakasam and Guntur.

A significant and perhaps the most controversial guideline stipulated in Project Tiger is the evacuation of all human habitations in the core areas. About 30 habitations are identified for evacuation in Srisailam-Nagarjun Sagar Tiger Sanctuary. From the Government's point of view (personal conversation with the conservator of forests and the field-director, Project Tiger) evacuation is necessary for the following reasons : (1) presence of human settlement in the Tiger areas is dangerous to the lives of people and cattle : (2) poaching by tribals endangers wild-life and would defeat the objective of the project : (3) evacuation of human settlements helps elimination of illegal trading (It is assumed that the tribals are responsible or are instrumental in illegal trading of hides and forest resources) ; (4) the core areas should be free from human interference so that natural equilibrium is safeguarded ; (5) the core areas serve as breeding nuclei for the Tiger and its perpetuation depends on non-interference from tribals : (6) human activity such as cultivation, food gathering and hunting upsets the natural equilibrium and new bio-chemical interactions are introduced due to the use of fertilizer and growing of modern crops.

About 30 Chenchu habitations are identified within the Srisailam-Nagarjuna Sagar Tiger Sanctuary. So far only three settlements are evacuated, one of which is Pechheruvu located in Atmakur sub-taluk of Kurnool district. The Chenchus of Pechhuruvu were evacuated in January 1986 and resettled in Palemcheruvu a small village on the plains adjacent to the villages of Hindu caste groups. This place is 32 km away from Pechheruvu.

The impact of Project Tiger and rehabilitation programmes on the Chenchus is presented in the following pages—an analysis of the functioning and policies of the Forest Department *vis-a-vis* the life-styles of the Chenchus. Fieldwork for this study was conducted in various phases during 1981-1986.

Forests, Wild-life and the Chenchu

Originally the Chenchu were food-gatherers and hunters. Today they are adopting wage-labour economy coupled with incipient annual dry farming. Forest and other administrative records have portrayed the Chenchu as criminals, drunkards and lazy people who would not contribute their labour to the 'deforestation' activities of the Forest Department. This opinion has not changed much among the officials of the present day bureaucratic organizations. The above opinion was, however, not corroborated by the anthropologists. Haimendorf vividly illustrates the simple life that the Chenchus lead in a manner their "stone age ancestors lived thousands of years ago" (1945 : VII). Another statement of Haimendorf is worth quoting here : "There can be no race in India poorer in earthly possessions than the Jungle Chenchu" (*ibid* : VII). It can be categorically stated that the Chenchus do not pose any threat to forest resources.

According to the written evidence, Chenchus inhabited the Nallamala forests since the 17th century (Buchanan, 1807). What was purely a nomadic population, roaming within the precincts of the Nallamala forests, the Chenchus have gradually established semi-permanent *gudem* (settlements) almost within the buffer zones or on the peripheral zones of the forest. The expanding agricultural populations of the neighbouring plain areas have pushed some of the Chenchu into interior forests and great extents of forests are felled down to convert into agricultural fields—an action which was supported both by the kingdoms, the British and to a certain extent by the Indian Government.

For the first time, the Nallamalai forests were opened to the wider world on a large scale by the British who laid down forest roads connecting several Chenchu *gudems.* The idea was to exploit Chenchu labour in the forestry activities and to create halting places for the forest personnel. However, the Chenchus depended upon the forests for their survival. They exploited the fruits, tubers, leaves and to a lesser extent herbivores,

The technology for hunting purpose was simple, use of bow and non-poisoned arrows. Floral species were exploited by the digging stick—another simple implement. The existence of virgin forests provided the Chenchus ample vegetarian food resources. Besides food the forest provided them medicinal herbs, honey and necessary equipment for shelter and technology.

The Chenchus have a vast knowledge of their environment. They tend to live in harmony with the forests without infringing the territories of the wild-life. The following points highlight the issue under consideration.

1. All *gudems* are erected quite far away from the water points, salt-lakes, grazing, preying and resting grounds of wild animals.
2. Hunting during nights, evenings and early mornings are traditionally avoided, for, the animals would be grazing or preying.
3. The Chenchus can identify the animals from foot-prints and faecal matter.
4. Avoidance of hunting of animals with cubs.
5. Safety mechanisms like shouting, drumming to drive away the wild animals especially the tiger. The Chenchus never challenge, tease or venture to kill tiger.
6. In a way the tiger provides food to the Chenchus. The latter scavenge over the kill of tiger.
7. The Chenchus exploit fully ripe season-specific food resources only. They avoid cutting or trampling the creepers and other plants which have some utility value.
8. Hunting frequency and success rate is very low.

The Chenchu have a clear perception of their surroundings which they divide into micro-environments of different wild-life (especially of tiger, bear, deer, and arboreal animals). To sum up, while the Chenchus wholly depended upon the forests for their sustenance, they had not faced any serious problem with the wild animals. Though stray instances of attack by the tiger are reported, maneaters are not encountered in the Nallamalai forests.

The Chenchus are timid, and shy. One of the most celebrated mechanisms of self-defence among the Chenchu is avoidance. The Chenchus would rather choose to vacate a place or their hut in the event of a misfortune, or dispute, instead of indulging in activities to face these situation. When the Chenchu spot a tiger roaming in a particular locality, they would not dare to visit those places. A Chenchu is so 'timid' that he would even stop his daily visits to the forests in search of food or wage-labour. However, the word "timidity" should not be construed as a psychological factor and lack of will. It should be understood basically as an adaptive mechanism so that friction or intrusion are avoided. It is basically oriented to achieve harmony among themselves and between themselves and the surrounding forest.

Forest policies

Forest policies have a tremendous impact on the life and culture of the Chenchus. A sense of alienation from the forests was forced upon the Chenchus by enacting the Forest Act of 1865 which stipulated absolute control over forests depriving all the customary rights of the local population. In the subsequent forest policies (1894, 1927, 1935) the control on and exploitation of forests were given thrust but certain concessions were allowed to the Chenchus. Nevertheless, the forest department exercised considerable control over the Chenchus by way of filing cases against them in terms of encroachment into reserved forests, oversize of the cattle herds, collection of Minor Forest Produce (MFP) from the prohibited tracts, thieving, hunting of animals, illicit distillation, cutting of bark for brewing, food collection, cultivation, *etc*. These policies as well as the post-Independence policies are tacitly aimed at discouraging the life-style that the Chenchu have been practising.

The ameliorative programmes and the "concessions" did not help the Chenchu. As a management strategy the rights to collect MFP were vested in a few individuals. Thus private rights over forest produce were developed against the previous norm of communal right which in turn disturbed the norm of collective consumption. Later on, even these rights were transferred to contractors and then to Girijan Cooperative Society. But private merchants remained and they collect more than 50% of MFP. The rights of the Chenchu have totally weaned out. Though the forest department has permitted the Chenchus to clear a plot of forest land for cultivation, no proper rights over there cultivable fields were so far conferred. In several instances the Chenchu were not allowed to cultivate these lands on the plea that all cultivable land fell under reserved forest area and hence cultivation of these lands was illegal.

Forest policies have helped the contractors and local merchants and are instrumental in the development of industries, business establishments and urban centres in the nearby places like district and taluk headquarters. There is a phenomenal increase in the number of timer depots, lorries and migrant labour in Dornala, Srisailam and Atmakur. But these benefits go only to a handful of people. Now the Forest Department does not care to employ the Chenchus for afforestation and deforestation activities due to the availability of transport facility and migrant labour. It is anybody's guess as to what extent the forest policies contributed to the environmental protection. It is truism that along with the legal trade, illegal trade has contributed to the deterioration of the environment. Monoculture of economically important species like teak and eucalyptus has destroyed the diversity of flora and fauna. The freedom to exploit the food resources from the forest, which the ancestors of the Chenchus did for generations, has been suppressed with an iron hand by the Forest Department. The Chenchus are largely left out as destitutes and made to depend on the government sponsored programmes.

It is against this background that the impact of Project Tiger should be evaluated. What follows is an account of Pechheruvu Chenchus who were evacuated and resettled at Palemcheruvu.

Rehabilitation Programme : The Case of Pechheruvu Chenchus

Pechheruvu is an ancient settlement inhabited by the Chenchu. Pechheruvu range has been identifieasd the chief breeding nucleus of the tiger. Some of the socio-economic and ecological characteristics of the Pechheruvu range are given below :

Total area of the range	: 98.14 sq. miles
Altitude of the plateau	: 2,000 ft.
Area of the settlement	: 5.00 acres
No. of water holes	: 9
No. of salt lakes	: 15
Extent of natural forest	: about 25 sq. miles
Type of forest	: Superior of deciduous and bamboo type forests
Communication	: Gravel road connecting the State highway
No. of Human settlements	: Permanent=1, camp sites=3
Population strength (as on December 1985)	: 375 individuals
No. of households	: 98
Amenities	: Elementary school, Girijan Cooperative Society, Forest Range Office, Women Welfare Centre
Area under cultivation	: 248 acres
Extent of area deforested	: 28 sq. miles
Extent of area afforested	: 9 sq. miles
Average annual net revenue	: about Rs. 60,000

The tiger had been a very familiar animal which the Chenchus of Pechheruvu used to encounter with a sense of condescension. The man-animal relationship was said to be very cordial. No cases of man-eaters were reported. Pechheruvu is also a place where the tiger lived without any interference from man. In fact, Pechheruvu is supposed to be a highly congenial breeding nucleus for tiger. The following features of Pechheruvu offer a congenial environment for the perpetuation of tiger population :

1. Existence of adequate area for free movement of the tigers ;

2. A small proportion of cultivable land and very low human population density ;
3. Existence of a relatively undisturbed area with plenty of prey species of varied types, especially deer, hares, *etc.*
4. Existence of a vast territory which facilitates groups of tigers and individual tigers to occupy separate territorial zones thereby minimizing the conflict between the tigers for safeguarding their territories ;
5. No intervention from the local populations (Chenchus) with the tigers and their territories ;
6. Presence of watersheds, openness of the jungle (which facilitates a stalking tiger to recognize his potential prey over long distances), presence of meadows where the prey species browse ;
7. Pechheruvu is surrounded by vast stretches of buffer zones where again population density is very low.

The major reason for evacuation is the idea that tiger reserve should be free from any kind of human interference. From the point of view of the Forest Department, absence of human populations completely removes several problems such as poaching, illegal trade, cattle-lifting and compensations, tiger attacks, disturbed environments uncongenial for quick propogation of the tigers, *etc.*

Some popular notions held by the Forest officials in support of the evacuation of human beings are listed as follows :

1. Tigers and men cannot share territories ;
2. Tigers need unmolested forests to perpetuate ;
3. Local people hate tigers, because the latter prey on their cattle ;
4. The Chenchu's view-point is ecologically shortsighted ;
5. Saving the tigers, and the forest it lives in, eventually provides many benefits to the villagers ;
6. Tigers do not voice but people do. Hence tigers are to be protected ;
7. Tigers do not create a scare and are not a meance but the Chenchu are ;
8. The fault lies with people but the tigers are always

made to pay which in turn leads the destructions of the forests ;

9. Chenchus are lazy and do not work (for the Forest Department). Tigers bring ecological equilibrium and income to the nation.

These statements fail to take into consideration the age-old life-styles which the Chenchus developed in harmony with nature. The Forest Department officials perceive the Chenchus as destroyers of forests which is not correct.

The Tiger Scare and Menace

The conflict between Tiger and the Chenchus seems to have started with the success of Project Tiger. It is estimated that nearly 93 tigers are inhabiting the Srisailam-Nagarjun Sagar Sanctuary. As the population of tigers increased, the problems of the Chenchus have also increased. The tigers started attacking the cattle, goats, dogs and people. In Pechheruvu alone 30 dogs, 68 cattle and 32 goats were killed by tigers. The Government has announced compensation for cattle-kills by Tigers. Not all cattle-kills are claimed by the owners and out of those cases which were brought to the notice of the officials, only ten cases were registered and only four cases were settled. The amount paid was very meagre, ranging from Rs. 200 to Rs. 750. The forest officials do not register a case unless proper evidence is produced. Many people could not provide proof because by the time officials were taken to the killing spot, the remains were already eaten away by a wild animal or the victims were dragged away by the tigers.

The tigers do not confine to the core areas. They move very freely, crossing the boundaries marked by the Wild-Life Act and inter cultural zones. Tigers have also attacked the Chenchu but no deaths were reported. Most of the attacks were simply case of mistaken identity especially during cutting grass, collecting tubers and firewood when the people lose their distinctive human look. Nevertheless, the Chenchu invoked their traditional means of coping with the tiger. They had understood the knack of avoiding a tiger. The following points illustrate the case in point :

programme. The strategy was to relocate individuals and not the community as such. This was the main force which induced a 'scatter effect' wherein most of the evicted Chenchus left to different places rather than staying at Palemcheruvu. Relocating individuals was easier than relocating communities. However, the Government has failed to utilize this theoretical premise in the Chenchu rehabilitation programme. The government failed to recognize that dislocating individuals from their traditional habitation amounts to a fundamental socio-cultural dislocation and weakens the local support structure which, as a community the people have built. Dislocating individuals had set in the effect of closed social system (Sudder, 1973, 51-53) upon the people. The Chenchus failed to cope up with the new situation. They could not establish links and networks with the populations and societies already residing in and around the new rehabilitation area. The Chenchus behaved as if they are highly isolated and closed to any outside interaction at the new place. Being 'timid' and 'shy' the Chenchu evacuees have not resorted to initiating innovations and adjust to the purely agriculture based social environment at the new place. The Chenchu evacuees also could not fit into the daily work rhythm at the new place, that starts quite early in the morning and ends late in the evening. The Chenchu are habituated to work only for a few hours during late forenoon and early afternoon.

The Chenchus had virtually no role to play in the local agrarian based social structure. The local people could not even 'exploit' the labour of the Chenchus, for, the latter lacked the requisite speed and skill in cultivation. There was no post-evacuation assessment or feed-back mechanism devised by the government. In these circumstances the Chenchu evacuees had adopted the security mechanism in order to cope up with the uncertainties and risks. The only alternative was to leave for their relative's settlements in order to hold fast to old behavioural patterns, old institutions and old lifestyles.

The most suitable approach would have been to distribute the Chenchu evacuees, depending on the settlers' selection, among the many Chenchu settlements located in the buffer zones by providing the same kind of physical assets which a household possessed at the time of eviction. Besides, providing certain incentives to the evacuees and public amenities at the places of resettlement would have increased the people's confidence both among themselves and in the government. The rehabilitation policy should make room for humanitarian component. Besides, the rehabilitation programme should be a dynamic process and should be executed in a carefully devised manner.

The myth of Natural Ecosystem without Human Interference

The total forest area falling under Pechheruvu range is 254.18 sq. km. Pechheruvu range is surrounded by other forest ranges the areas of which amounts to a total of 1558.38 sq. km. The total area covered under Project Tiger was 3568 sq. km. Large scale fellings are undertaken 1860 onwards, throughout the Nallamalai. Virgin forests are now confined to valleys and hill slopes. Bamboo forests are almost destroyed after awarding contracts to Siripur Paper Mills and Rayalaseema Paper Mills. Demand for forest resources has also increased enormously. Demand for gum was so great that hundreds and thousands of trees were destroyed. Haimendorf (1982) makes an extremely valid point when he writes that cutting of bamboo was so unscientific that regeneration is curbed. So is the case with collection of gum and timber. This is the case when the migrant labourers are employed.

Large scale deforestation activities led to afforestation where monoculture is given priority over growing natural floral species like Chirumanu (*Onogeissue latifolia*), Nallamalai (*Terminalia tomentosa*), Yepi (*Hardwickis*) and a score of other important trees having value for timber, fodder, and food. Monocropping has serious implications for the environment. While no authentic evaluation studies exist to determine the success of afforestation activities, it is a truism that afforestation policies would not create an ecological equilibrium. The fact that the afforestation activities are oriented towards reaping commercial benefits is a testimony for the above contention. Notwithstanding the role of "sorcerer's apprentice" to create an ecological equilibrium by way of afforestation activities, the Government introduced yet another scheme under a catchy title Project Tiger symbolizing our technocratic non-culture which considers all costs except human and that too, of the tribal. Long term implications of the project are not clearly specified.

Though all types of forest exploitation is banned in the core areas, unabated illegal as well as large scale legal felling and other types of exploitation is progressing in the buffer zones with increased vigour. The vested interests have assumed such a magnitude of conflicting priorities that no proper organizational linkages exist between the three branches of the Forest Department *viz.* Forest Development Corporation, Wild-Life Department and the Forest Department (General). Predictably each organ is at loggerheads with one another blaming each other, politicians and the Chenchus about the ills of the whole issue of forest environment.

Under these circumstances one wonders about the logic of keeping man and tiger apart to realize the major objective of achieving natural ecological equilibrium.

The Real Options and Priorities

The idea that existing forest areas of country should be protected for maintenance of ecological balance may have its significance and validity. It is on the basis of the above premise that the government is initiating uprooting of people in Nallamalai. But the underlying scientific validity and the contention of environmental protection cannot form the basis for justification regarding eviction of people. The existing socio-economic and political issues are to be taken into consideration before the eviction of people from their original habitats.

Given the life-styles and the indigenous mechanisms to cope with the various problems including tiger in their own environment, evicting the Chenchus seems to be yet another folly of the planners. The growing menace from the tiger could be averted by various modern mechanisms. For instance a strong cattle shed to accommodate all the cattle of the settlement would be an ideal mechanism to contain tiger attacks. Actually no study was undertaken to explore the reasons behind the tiger visits to Chenchu settlements in search of cattle. The tiger are highly prone to attack cattle by way of habit which, if it proved so, needed to be corrected irrespective of evacuation or no evacuation. In Sunderbans man-eating is now being discouraged by means of erecting clay mannequins which give 230 volts shock upon contact. The same experiment could be even undertaken at Nallamalai. Besides, all the Chenchu settlements can be shielded from tiger attacks by erecting a strong fence. On the other hand if eviction becomes necessary, the Chenchus should not be displaced out of their forest environments. The Government should endeavour to create large extents of buffer zones and reclaim barren and destroyed bushy lands into forest areas. The Forest Department should reverse the whole historical process of exploitation of forests. The Forest Department should trust the poor Chenchus and treat them as human beings. The buffer zones and peripheral regions of the forests should be safeguarded for a realistic and serious afforestation programmes for growing local species. The Chenchu should be involved in planning and in forest management. They should be educated about the modern techniques of preserving and conservation of forests and economic aspects of forest resources.

REFERENCES

BUCHANAN G. F. (1807), *A Journey from Madras Through Mysore, Canara and Malabar*, London.

FURER-HAIMENDORF, C. VON. (1945), "Tribal Populations of Hyderabad : Yesterday and Today". (in) *Census of India 1941*, Vol. XXI, Part I—Report, Hyderabad : Government Central Press.

FURER- HAIMENDORF, C. VON. (1982) *Tribes of India*. Delhi : Oxford University Press.

SASTRY, V.N.V.K. (1984), "Institutionalized Encroachment on Man-Nature Relationship and Impact on Primitive Tribal Groups". *Development Strategy : Primitive Tribal Groups* (eds) Asoke Kumari Tigidi and K. Mohan Rau. Hyderabad : Tribal Cultural Research and Training Institute.

SCUDDER, T. (1973), "The Human Ecology & Big Projects : River Basin Development and Resettlement" in *Annual Review of Anthropology* (eds) Bernard J. Seigel, Alan R. Beals and Stephen A. Tyler. Vol 2, California ; Annual Review Inc.

[illegible]

[illegible] could be [illegible] from [illegible] On the other hand [illegible] Government [illegible]

[illegible] Department should cover the whole [illegible] The Forest Department [illegible] should be regarded [illegible] and second [illegible] The Chambers should [illegible] and economic aspects of [illegible]

REFERENCES

[illegible]

5

Loktak Project and Some Basic Issues for the Communities in Manipur Valley

B.M. Mukherjee*

Introduction

Rehabilitation problems in industrialization are quite common and more of a serious nature in tribal areas and remote places. The activities of development and industrialization have affected the quality, the environment and created problems like family disorganization, pollution, soil erosion, and destruction of wild life. In the present study I have found that the quality of life of the affected families have gone down beyond imagination. The findings are based on anthropological fieldwork conducted by the author on a small group of 20 families living near the Loktak hydro-electricity project, situated at about 30 kms. south of Imphal town in Manipur. Other supplementary information were collected from six families

*Associate Professor, Department of Anthropology, Manipur University, Canchipur, Imphal-795 003.

who had to leave their ancestral place in order to find an alternative. This study was carried out in early 1987 just to bring to light the impact of developmental processes in the remotest areas of the country. And as such the present article brings out many new issues regarding the local population who had to face dire consequences.

Tools and Techniques

The data, qualitative in nature were collected through close observation and unstructured interviews. A sample of 26 households was chosen of which 20 families may be considered fortunate because they somehow managed to adjust with the new environment. Seven informants belonging to senior generations had to be contacted for they could narrate the past history and their experiences.

Area and the Ethnic Group

Topographically, Manipur falls into two distinct natural regions—the Central Valley and the Hills surrounding it. The hills are predominantly inhabited by various tribes except in certain pockets with conspicuous concentration of non-tribal population. The valley is predominently inhabited by the Meiteis, the Muslims, the Scheduled Castes of Lois and the Scheduled Tribes. The area under study is a part of the valley where the tribes mostly Kabuis, Rongmeis and a sprinkling of other religious or community groups inhabit. Some 8 kms. away from this area is situated a historical place known as Moirang and to its eastern side at a distance of 3 kms one can find a beautiful and very big lake known a Loktak lake. There are residential quarters for the employees of the Loktak project and in and around this area there are many settlements and family clusters. So this Loktak complex is now a heterogeneous area. People from diverse ethnic, linguistic and cultural origin have come together at one place. There are Biharis, Bengalis, South Indians, tribals, Meiteis, Muslims and others. Before 1972 there were only the Manipuris and the tribals who depended on agriculture, fishing, carpentry, basketry, gathering, spinning, weaving and embroidery, small trade in the local markets, *etc.*, for their subsistence. All these three groups *i.e.*, the Meitei, the Muslim, the Loi and the Tribals are historically known for their peaceful coexistence and come out to help each other at the time of crisis. In most of the families the married sons lived with their parents. But since 1972 things have started changing with the commencement of the construction work for the project.

Spatial and Economic displacement

Historically, the tribals, the Meiteis, the Muslims of Loktak and Moirang area were subsisting chiefly with cultivation and limited variety of forest produce, hunting, fishing and the practice of rudimentary crafts. Near the project site there are some scattered families forming clusters who belong either to peasantry or to tribal group. The Meitei families practised settled cultivation while the tribals had been doing hill cultivation on the foothills. Side by side they were engaged in home-based industries, such as weaving and embroidery of cheap cotton and woollen clothes, making of fishing nets, mats, baskets, wood-work, *etc.*, apart from raising of live-stock. Household industries have been exclusively women's responsibility apart from their domestic duties. Market is also controlled by women and the selling of commodities, vegetable vending, supply of eggs and milk are the other areas of economic activity. The places around Loktak and Moirang have maintained a distinct style of life in the sense that some of the classical themes, cultural traits and elements are still being preserved by the people and live like an encysted group within the community.

There is no evidence of spatial displacement because the setttlements were not disturbed and their removal did not happen in this case. But there were as many as six tribal families who could not survive due to ecological changes and migrated to further southward hill region of Churachandpur. It was reported by the members of this group that they were affected indirectly by the construction of Loktak project and the abrupt changes warranted the people to run away from here. Further, it was explored by adopting non-formal interview method, that they continued to be virtually isolated till 1971 and have very little political, educational and economic aspirations or connection with the outer world. These families in the beginning sought to maintain a *status quo*, but failed to do so due to the increase of population and changes in the physical environment. Under the changing situation it appeared very difficult for them to find out the means of livelihood. Streams and rivulets would no longer provide them small fishes. The small hills and hedges where they used to go for hunting small animals and for collection of fuel, fruits, vegetables and fodder suddenly disappeared. The raw materials for their arts and crafts bamboos, timber tree bark, grass, *etc.*, were no more in sight. The authorities of the project acquired a vast stretch of land over which the common people were not allowed to move freely. On the other hand, they had no alternative means of survival. The technological innovation failed to provide the tribals even a small share of developmental benefits. On the contrary, the process of change in the economy, rate of monetization and ecological and socio-cultural adaptation by other groups were so rapid that these families fell flat and had no other go than abandoning their ancestral place. Government of Manipur and the local administration remained unconcerned since no acquisition of settled land had taken place. In this way the poor people silently moved out of this area without making their absence felt.

Adjustment Problems

Now we will take up the case of 20 families who somehow dared to confront the adverse situation brought about by the introduction of the said project. Excepting two tribal families, all belonged to either Meitei or Muslim peasantry. With the process of change people started to have their own conflicting interests and ambivalent attitude which they only whispered among themselves but never beyond their ethnic group. Some of the village/community level meetings convened at the initiative of the traditional leaders and local political leaders at a later stage. Efforts were made to organise the local people with a view to safeguarding the interest of the members and demand the share of the fruits of techno-economic development. As a response to this only eight families could receive the irrigational facilities for their roadside paddy lands. Others proposed for employment opportunities and subsequently twelve members from this group were employed. Of these employees ten young men are working as unskilled workers/peons and two engaged in clerical job. A few families have started petty business like grocery, tea stalls and *pan* shops under the care and supervision of their women. From as long back as 1974 the indigenous population started adjusting with the new environment. The people who were indifferent so far started making adjustments in trying to get some benefit. The local women began to go from door to door as vegetable vendors. The colony has enabled them to find clients.

In and around the project site now it has taken-the shape of a semi-industrialized small town constituted by various people of diverse ethnic and cultural origin. There are employees, shop-keepers, original inhabitants, outsiders who interact with each other in various ways. Most of the technical personnel have come from outside the state. In this context it will be worthwhile to analyse some of the basic issues related to their economy, rituals and festivals, institutions, traditions and inter-group relations.

First of all let us pry into their economic condition. The economy of the local people has certainly some impact of the new industrial climate. The families have become conscious of the monetary economy and a sense of gainful employment is gradually gaining ground. This has helped in making them aware of labour cost. Unlike the earlier stage of hand-to-mouth economy today they are slightly better off. In other words the monthly salary system has indeed left a positive impact in the minds of the local inhabitants to look for into the future. A few family heads may be found discussing about the family budgets which was quite unusual earlier. Money lending business does no longer draw the clients. Many instances of occupational mobility, particularly, inter-generational type may be found today.

On the other side there has been many harmful effects of this change. Mutual help and cooperation for each other at the time of need has completely disappeared. Unity and solidarity questions come up only when there is an attempt to integrate socio-politically the Manipuri speaking people. Needs of the families have been multiplied as a result of adding many luxury items in their day-to-day life. The craze for such things is so much that they are ready to possess the items of their choice by adopting any means—may be fair or foul. Cent per cent people have the habit of drinking and many young men have become drug addicts. The Meiteis who had religious taboo for certain non-vegetarian food items no longer do so. In dress and ornaments they look like any other Indian and at time difficult to identify their culture and language. The institution of *Marup* which used to maintain structural-functional cohesion has gone a long way in converting it into a downgraded institution of lottery and gambling which at present may be considered an instrument of exploitation. Class consciousness has been emerging out of the economic inequality and accumulation of wealth and property disproportionate to the individual income. Bribery is quite rampant and a new class of exploiters is coming up very fast.

Coming to the ritual-religious life of the people it was felt and perceived that this aspect has remarkably declined. Religious taboo, observing fast, religious sentiments are no longer associated with male members. Only the ceremonial aspects of family functions and festivals exist. *Thouba-chouba, Cherouba* and other festivals and also the *Swasthi Puja*, the function at the birth of a child on the sixth day are no longer being observed with the ritual sanctity, sentiment and purity of mind. These rituals and festivals have been reduced to the level of entertainment, feast and sensual pleasure. Instead some of the great traditional festivals, like, *Holi, Diwali etc.*, are being celebrated with gusto along with the outsiders and the harmful elements of these festivities have been absorbed in the local traditions.

Some of the classical institutions and traditions have gone to the background and the cultural values and norms one can hardly trace out. The family size is becoming smaller. There is not much care towards the rearing of children, economic security for women and old persons. Some institutions that helped in socializations and acculturation of members are fast receding to the background. Folk-lores, folk-songs, art that contributed to non-formal education are on the wane. In place of elopement marriages the young men and women now prefer to go along the path of love marriage and courtship. Age-grade distinction is non-existent resulting in disrespect and disregard to senior members. This has brought a pernicious effect on the interpersonal relationship which may be held responsible for family disharmony and disorganization which occur frequently. The institution of *Ashiba Marup* (financial safeguard for the families enabling them to perform death rituals and funeral feasts) does not seem to continue as strong as it was before. There is a constant flow of harmful elements and ideas from outside into the formely encysted community. At times the conflict between the traditional ritual-based religious leader or village leader and the modern secular political leader may be easily observed and noticed. Mushrooming of English medium schools have given opportunities to the members of upper class for the minting of money. Sending the children to these schools has remained only a status symbol. The Manipuri medium schools on the other hand are unable to draw students from the families who have come up above the subsistence level of economy. That means those who can afford tuition fee have the inclination of sending their children to the English schools. So the poor families only send their children to the Government schools and the teachers do not take interest. On the other hand, the English medium schools have miserably failed as the children are neither motivated nor inspired to learn anything except the English manners. So a class of under-qualifieds is produced by these schools.

Discussion and Conclusion

In spite of the fact that various ethnic groups from diverse origin and different languages are living together for more than fifteen years, the gap between the *Mayangs* and the *Manipuris* has not yet reduced and rather it has become-wider. The relationship between the outsiders and the local people has deteriorated lately characterized by the unfavourable attitude and ill-will toward each other. The children of the two communities seldom become friends. Sometimes the situation becomes tense as the original inhabitants start feeling that the outsiders are responsible for their economic and cultural deprivation.

As stated earlier there was no acquisition of the agricultural or residential holdings but the six tribal families were compelled to Churachandpur. The reason for leaving the ancestral homes may be attributed to the cultural and ecological imbalance. These families have not yet been able to establish themselves in a new area. And therefore they have gone back to a state of more primitivism in terms of food procurement, technology and economy. They are unable to receive basic facilities and amenities as the new location is far from the town area. It was revealed that even after a period of twelve years there is no increase in the population. On further inquiry it came to notice that the health standard of women and children has considerably fallen. Male members of these families are not able to find meaningful occupation and as a result suffer from loss of energy and idleness. Now we will go back to the project complex and examine the local people in the process of adjustment. The impact of development process may certainly be traced out but the output is negative. The population has a retarded growth. The broad areas of change may be summarised as under :

1. The first group who abandoned the area had virtually refused any change and preferred to live their own life taking least interest in political, cultural and economic aspirations or connections with the outer world (tribals).
2. The second group is formed by those who are employed in the project and somehow have emulated the traditions of other's culture and gone so far that it may to social organization in near future. In due course of time their local traditions may completely be destroyed leading to a point of no return.
3. The third group is represented by the population who have received a small share of the benefit of development directly or indirectly to maintain their subsistence. They are conscious of maintaining and preserving their cultural autonomy and have sought to identify themselves with a great tradition or have riddled with the

problem of solidarity-emulation complex, or technology-ritual conflict.

Taking a cue from the processes and direction of change and also the reactions of the people to the development projects we are now in a position to examine the problems. Displacement does not always mean migration from one place to another. There are other meanings of displacement also. As in this case the communities suffered most due to their economic and cultural displacement. Even if the management may not be held directly responsible for the displacement of six families but the force to oust them was so strong that they were compelled to run away. Therefore, the Government was partly responsible for creating an atmosphere detrimental to the cultural and economic life of the people.

Before the construction of such projects the people of the area have to be systematically motivated. There is an urgent need to share the culture of science and technology by the people and this necessitates setting up of science training camps. In this regard a congenial atmosphere must be created and it is always desirable that some local leaders have to be taken into confidence. A technical training course for the inhabitants for a short period might prove helpful. A thorough and systematic study of the people and culture surrounding the project area must be conducted with the help of professional anthropologists so that the attitudes, interests, feelings and barriers of development are clearly understood. It is also required that the cultural isolation of certain groups be maintained until they develop human adaptive capacities for living in a world of change. Those who are in a position to receive and absorb some of the cultural elements and traits from outside the encysted community must be made aware of the merits and demerits. That is, the development of right attitude and awareness to the interrelationship between culture, nature and technology are the prerequisites. Knowledge gained through this would invariably resolve problems.

Finally it must be made clear that the question of rehabilitation would come up not only for those people who have been rendered homeless after acquisition of their agricultural or residential holdings, but also for those who were affected economically or culturally by the development schemes and processes. It is not as simple as it seems to examine these issues because it goes a long way. The matter does not end just after the payment of compensation in cash or by way of arranging another settlement. For some time the community in question must be kept under close observation until they resume their normal duties. The Government should also invest capital for opening up cottage industries for the local people in and around Loktak. For instance in this case the communities have expressed their keen interests to start poultry, piggery, embroidery, spinning and weaving, wood carving, bamboo and cane industry, fruits, vegetables and fish preserving units, women's cooperative societies, market centres, dance and drama centres, sports and athletics promotion centres *etc.* Along with these preoccupations the community would gradually march forward. This will help in maintaining a balance between the components of traditional culture and the components of modern science and technology and finally receive the fruits of development with the healthy growth of individual groups.

6

River Dam Projects and Rehabilitation Planning : A Profile of project affected populations of Jayakwadi and Srisailam Projects

P. Sudhakara Reddy*

India is the most important dam building nation in the world. In the larger interest of the nation, to fulfil irrigational and electricity needs and help control floods, 1,500 multipurpose reservoirs have been built in the country. Over a third of all these dams are in the State of Maharashtra. These dams are today India's most controversial socio-cultural and environmental issues creating many problems such as social disorganisation rehabilitation of the displaced population, loss of forest cover, increased pressure on agricultural lands, increased water-borne diseases, salinisation of agricultural lands, siltation and so on. The displacement of populations from their traditional habitat and the consequent exposure to new cultural

*Department of Social Anthropology, Sri Venkateswara University, Tirupati.

milieu, have created many problems for both the affected populations and the administration.

Social scientists have studied the displaced and uprooted communities as a result of constructions and establishments such as steel plants, national parks, hydro-electric and irrigation projects, *etc.* (Roy Burman, B.K., 1968 ; Vidyarthi, L.P., 1970 ; Sarkar, J.C., 1970 ; Muthaiah, B.C. and Mathur, J.S., 1975 ; Reddy, P.S., 1981 ; Karve, I., 1967 ; Joshi, B.L., 1982 ; Joshi, V., 1983 ; Sawant, P.R., 1985). Most of the studies deal with displacement the ways in which compensation amount was spent, rehabilitation and resettlement programmes, the socio-economic conditions before and after the displacement, the problems of the affected populations, and also give suggestions for the welfare of the affected. The nature and problems of displacement and rehabilitation programmes of the river dam projects differ from the displacement and rehabilitation programmes of the other large constructions in some aspects such as, getting employment opportunities, areas of urban growth utilisation of old acquired lands, *etc.*

The major issue in the construction of large river dams is not nature but people. Usually these populations are tribals and peasants, mostly the poorest and the most powerless. Even if the planners grant compensation in the form of land elsewhere, they fail to realise the emotional and socio-cultural attachment that people have to their ancestral homes. The displaced populations could not adjust to the new setting and returned to areas close to where they originally lived after abandoning the rehabilitation colonies and selling the newly allotted land.

The present study deals with the planning of rehabilitation and resettlement programmes among the affected populations of large river dams, *viz.* Jayakwadi in Maharashtra and Srisailam in Andhra Pradesh. The data for the study were collected from secondary sources such as official records and also through fieldwork conducted among the project affected populations of Srisailam during 1984-85, and of Jayakwadi during June-July, 1988.

The knowledge about the socio-economic aspects of the affected villages of Jayakwadi and Srisailam projects, before their displacement helps us to understand the ways of life of the different sections of the affected populations. The affected villages which were multi-caste and primarily based on agriculture, consisted of the peasant castes, the artisan castes and the service castes including the unclean castes. They were mutually depending on *jajmani* type of relations. Majority of the population were illiterate.

The displaced villages of both the projects were located on river banks, the soil was black and very fertile and was cultivable for both Rabi and Kharif. Most of the families had land and the families without land were in agricultural labour, household industry, petty trade, artisans and other services. People who were close to each other in the social system lived side by side, people whose social positions were widely different lived apart. The temples and other sacred places of the respective religious groups were situated in the respective residential areas of these religious groups. The size and structure of the houses of different caste groups varied and the cultivators had larger houses than the other occupational groups. Kinship, caste and locality in general were the determinants of interpersonal and inter-group relations (Joshi, B.L., 1982). In most of the villages, any matter of dispute was handled by the senior members of the respective castes or villages to which the parties or persons at dispute belonged. The inter-caste relations were cordial and reciprocal.

The Jayakwadi irrigation project was constructed on the Godavari river near Paithan, a small town in Aurangabad district of Maharashtra. The project was started in 1965 and after its completion it was dedicated to the nation on 24-2-1976. The reservoir created by the dam, which is named as 'Nathsagar,' has submerged 35,000 hectares of land covering 96 multi-caste and agro-based villages with a population of 77,000. These villages have been shifted and rehabilitated at safer places. Fifty villages in Aurangabad district, and 46 villages in Ahmednagar district were affected fully or partially.

The Srisailam hydro-electric project was constructed across the river Krishna near Srisailam, in Kurnool district of Andhra Pradesh. Work on the project was started in 1963 and the first 110 M.W. unit was commissioned in 1983. The project has submerged 52 villages in Kurnool district and 65 villages in Mahabubnagar district, displacing over one lakh people and inundating 1,06,925 acres of dry and wet land and 20,728 households.

The affected people in both the projects faced various problems such as inadequate compensation, inordinate delay in payment of compensation, misdeeds of the concerned officials in fixing and payment of compensation, and the problems faced due to improper planning for rehabilitation programmes.

The extent of damages to the affected villages of both the projects varies and accordingly they are classified into four categories, *viz.* (a) complete village and its lands affected, (b) village and its lands partially affected, (c) only village lands affected partially and (d) only village affected partially. The families in 24 villages under the Jayakwadi project and 27 villages under the Srisailam project were fully affected losing both the houses and lands and are the worst sufferers compared to the partialy affected villages.

Due to displacement most of the affected populations have lost their traditional eco-social and cultural system. The evacuation programme was linked with rehabilitation programme. For the Jayakwadi affected populations, the rehabilitation centres were selected with the help of villages advisory committees. Most of the partialy and fully affected villagers preferred and resettled in nearby places. Very few of the fully affected villages were rehabilitated in command area. Land was acquired, layouts were prepared, and the plots were distributed to the displaced families by the revenue department. The infrastructure and civic amenities such as construction of internal and approach roads, provision of drinking water, construction of school, chavadies, panchayat office *etc.* was undertaken by the Zilla Parishad for every rehabilitation centre. Housing loans were provided to the displaced for the construction of houses. The Government has also provided land in CADA to a few of the displaced families. The District Collector has issued PAPs (Project Affected Populations) certificate to those fully affected populations who could not get land. With this certificate, they can get land in any district of Maharashtra depending on the availability of government lands. Besides, the government have also provided 5% of the vacancies as reservation in the government and semi-government services to the PAPs.

In the case of the Srisailam project, the evacuation programme was a man-made disaster as the government vacated the people through summary demolitions and police force in May, 1981. The people were not informed properly or educated sufficiently about the details of evacuation. The government have not provided rehabilitation centres but has just given rehabilitation cash grant. The main reason in delaying their evacuation was the lack of alternate house sites/rehabilitation centres. The grant of displacement money of Rs. 50/- was to meet food expenses at the time of actual evacuation. Rehabilitation cash grants were paid only to those who owned property. The evacuees had to go on their own initiative to purchase house sites in areas nearer to the old villages for their resettlement. House sites were provided only to a few and mostly the evacuees were not satisfied as they were invariably inaccessible. However, the government has provided some civic amenities such as provision of school, panchayat office, electricity, roads *etc.* in the new villages. In Andhra Pradesh there was no independent directorate to look after the rehabilitation programmes as in Maharashtra.

The physical, emotional and sentimental issues involved in forced migration have to be understood sensitively and the problem tackled with patience. The project affected populations prefer occupational and individual rehabilitation rather than the mere provision of infrastructure in the rehabilitation colonies or new villages. In both the project affected populations about 90% of the partialy affected populations and about 60% of the fully affected populations including those who settled in distant areas were resettled mostly in the areas nearer to the old villages. Most of the villages were resettled in toto. The affected population who scattered and resettled in distant places are very few.

The government have failed to realise the emotional and cultural attachment the displaced people have to their ancestral homes. In the case of most of the dams, the displaced people returned to areas close to where they originally lived after abandoning the rehabilitation centres. As the problems of displacement and rehabilitation do not fall into their court, designers and planners are not readily concerned. The study of rehabilitation and resettlement pattern of the affected populations in both the projects, and other river dam projects, shows that most of the fully and partialy affected populations preferred and resettled in the areas nearer to their old villages, with an intention of cultivating their old lands whenever the water level of the reservoir decreased.

The following measures are suggested for the planning of displacement and rehabilitation programmes of river dam projects :

(1) to prepare plan proposals of displacement and rehabilitation along with the plan proposals of the construction project,

(2) a thorough study of socio-economic conditions and attitudes of the population to be affected, to understand their ways of life for proper rehabilitation,

(3) to educate the population to be affected, in advance, about the importance of the project and detailed information of their proposed displacement and rehabilitation,

(4) to pay adequate compensation,

(5) to create a high power autonomous body to design and implement the programmes and to establish a separate directorate of rehabilitation and to coordinate and execute the programmes carefully,

(6) to make the affected population to participate in the planning and implementation programmes through rehabilitation advisory committees at different levels,

(7) to design and implement the rehabilitation programmes to suit their old socio-cultural and ecological setting,

(8) to link the payment of compensation to the rehabilitation programmes to spend the compensation amount in a meaningful way,

(9) to circulate a detailed final report on the displacement

and rehabilitation programmes among the populations to be affected,

(10) to handle the programmes of displacement and rehabilitation carefully and patiently or through the voluntary organizations (Narmada Valley Project),

(11) to provide rehabilitation centres nearer to their old villages or in CADA area only,

(12) to provide occupational rehabilitation or individual rehabilitation rather than communal or village rehabilitation with the provision of civic amenities only.

REFERENCES

JOSHI, B.L. (1982), Displacement and Rehabilitation : Study of a Dam Affected Rural Community, Parimal Prakashan, Aurangabad.

JOSHI, (1983), Resettlement of Submerged Villages, Centre for the Study of Social Sciences, Surat.

GOLDSMITH, & HILDYARD, N. (1985), The Social and Environmental Effects of Large Dams, Wade Bridge Ecological Centre.

Lokayan Research Programme of the Centre for the Study of Developing Societies, Delhi. (1981) A Report of the Fact Finding Committee.

7

Industrial Development and Problems of the Uprooted : A Case Study

I. Udaya Bhaskara Reddy*

Introduction

In a country like ours where an overwhelming majority of people live in rural areas and are ridden with chronic poverty, widespread unemployment and underemployment, subsistence production, poor marketing, communication and transport facilities, the initiation of large industries and other developmental projects will play a vital link in the overall development of the country.

The developmental activities initiated in the post-independence period for the coordinated development of rural areas had given an opportunity for the establishment of large developmental projects such as industries, irrigation, power and other non-traditional activities. These developmental activities are purposive planned interventions for accelerating economic development of the country and thereby reducing the regional

*Tata Institute of Social Sciences, Deonar, Bombay-400088,

imbalances over a period of time. Thus the main objective along with balanced regional development has been to uplift the local people who mostly consist of economically weaker sections, *viz.* scheduled castes, tribes and other landless labourers by providing them with employment and other social and economic benefits. These development projects have become symbols of national development, because these are usually implemented in backward, tribal and remote rural areas, where modern development is yet to be initiated. The people living in these areas look at these developments with high hopes. These projects have potential in solving various problems of rural areas such as generation of employment opportunities, skill development, increase in income and consumption, improvement of transport, communication and other infrastructural facilities, modifications in the cultural patterns, changes in social values and other traditional organisations. However, these developmental efforts are not unmixed blessings. Though they created several benefits, these projects also caused various social and economic disasters like widespread displacement of people from their habitats and occupations, and led to several environmental problems.

In India, after independence, great stress has been laid on industrialisation to achieve a balanced development. This had given a scope for the exploitation of vast natural resources like bauxite, coal, aluminium, manganese, *etc.* and this process had led to the establishment of large industries in different parts of rural India. Since independence, a number of industries such as steel plants at Jamshedpur, Rourkela, Bhilai, Durgapur and Bokaro, Heavy Engineering Corporation at Ranchi, Bharat Heavy Electricals Ltd. at Ramachandrapuram, Coal Mines at Dhanbad and Hazaribag, Cement factories at Jhinkpuri and Ranjanaguda, Fertilizer factory at Talcher have come up in backward tribal areas. All these industries have displaced people from their habitats and occupations. A conservative estimate indicates that about 20 lakh people were displaced due to the establishment of industries in the past and out of these only 6.50 lakh people are rehabilitated (Das, *et al*, 1988 : 274). In most cases the uprooted people are usually tribals and other economically weaker sections of the society. It is estimated that the proportion of tribals displaced by the development projects varied between (52 to 100 per cent Reddy, 1989 : 5). These people are forced to sacrifice their interests and sentiments attached to their traditional villages, houses and land in the larger interest of the society and nation. Thus industries have proved to be good for the nation, but for the tribals it has proved to be disastrous and created several problems in the process of their readjustment in the new environment.

A Case Study of NALCO Industrial Complex

The discovery of over one billion tonnes of bauxite deposited on the east coast of India has brought about a dramatic change in the country's potential as one of the leading producer of bauxite and aluminium. This had given a scope for the setting up of one of the world's leading aluminium complex, National Aluminium Company Limited (NALCO) in Koraput district of Orissa. The establishment of NALCO in an underdeveloped tribal area like Koraput provided a scope for creating employment opportunities improving the living standards of local people who are mostly tribals and other backward people and enables them to become conscious of self-development in respect of economic, social, educational and psychological status. This will also provide scope for the flow of wide range of other small and ancillary industries and stimulate the pace of economic growth and transform the life of the people in this region. The establishment of NALCO is one of the major landmarks in industrial self-sufficiency offering employment to several people providing scope for the local people and improving the infrastructural facilities in backward tribal areas. However, this project has acquired 3,444 hectares of land and will displace 2,368 persons in 15 villages, while another 736 persons in four villages will be affected by land acquisition (Muthayya, *et. al*, 1984 ; 2). This will affect the uprooted people seriously. Against the backdrop of the foregoing observations, the present paper analyses the positive benefits as well as problems created by the project to the uprooted people and then suggests certain guidelines for their planned rehabilitation.

Impact on Traditional Economy

Initiation of large industrial projects in backward tribal areas is an important phase in economic development seeking to increase, improve and diversify the productive capacities and thereby raising the living standards of local people. It also means a qualitative change of an economy, alteration in the existing skills and the introduction of new techniques to enable the people to diversify their occupations into industrial activities (Vidyarthi, 1970 : 1-2). One of the important benefit created by the project is change in the occupational pattern of the people. The changing occuptional structure in the project area is presented in Table 1 below.

TABLE 1

Occupational Structure of the Uprooted People in NALCO Project Area (1984-85)

(in percentage)

Occupation	SC/ST (N—313)	Caste Hindus (N—246)	Total (N—559)
Cultivators/ Agricultural labourers	6.1	16.7	10.7
Casual labourers	72.2	58.9	66.4
Service in projects and other establishments	10.2	16.3	12.9
Petty business	2.2	4.1	3.0
Others	9.3	4.1	7.0

The comparison of occupational structure in the project area with that of district's figure shows that while more than three fourths (82%) of the district's working population are engaged in agricultural activities, either as cultivators or agricultural labourers, only 11 per cent in the project area are engaged in similar occupations. Owing to proximity of industry and availability of different kinds of jobs, a number of people are engaged either as permanent employees in the project or casual workers in various project works. Thus it is observed that two-thirds are casual workers working under contractors in house building, road and bridge construction, *etc.* Further, about 13 per cent are employed as watchmen, helpers, *mazdoors* and sweepers in the project. According to the latest information available, out of 375 displaced households as on October 1988, 279 households (74.4%) are provided permanent jobs in the project. The nature of these jobs includes driver, plumber, pump operator, helper, attendant, *mazdoor*, *etc.* Thus there is a transformation in the occupational structure of uprooted activities to non-traditional industrial jabs. The other important benefit created by the project is raise in the income level. The income pattern in the project area is shown in Table 2 below.

TABLE 2

Details of Household Income among Uprooted people in NALCO Project Area (1984-85)

Income Details	SC/ST (N=146)	Caste Hindu (N=104)	Total (N=250)
Average income/ household per year (Rs)	6059.00	7138.00	6508.C0
Average earner per household	2.30	2.14	2.24
Average income per earning member (Rs)	2634.00	3335.00	2905.00
Per capita income (Rs)	1314.00	1653.00	1453.00

The NALCO project has provided a scope for raising the earning and purchasing capacity of local people and a large section of people are benefited due to direct and indirect employment opportunities. Besides creating about 6300 direct jobs, the project would also create about 20,000 job opportunities through ancillary industries, transport contact, shopping complexes *etc* (Reddy and Chattopadhyay, 1987 : 3). Thus the indirect employment opportunities are very substantial and the project has blessed the local people with raised and secured income. In addition it has also provided a ready market for selling their products and thus raised the earning capacity. As a result the income pattern has also undergone changes. The per capita income which is reported to be Rs. 1453 is much higher than the national figure, only Rs. 775 during 1984-85 (Sreenivasan, 1987 : 10-11). Thus it may be concluded that one of the striking contributions of the NALCO project is improving the living standards of uprooted as well as local people.

In addition the surrounding villages in the project area have opened up to the outside world and it has become easy for them to catch the pace of development taking place outside. The project also created strong market force for their own demand of different consumer items and this in turn has helped the project area to emerge as a regional market with much larger service area beyond the limits of the complex. Further, a number of service and business units of different categories have also come up to cater to the daily needs of the people in the project and periphery areas and thus opened a scope for self-employment avenues and also created good market for local agricultural products. Besides, various amenities such as education, health, banks, *etc.* have also been established to cater to the needs of the people working in the project and the people around the project area are becoming more conscious of availing these facilities.

Although the project created certain positive benefits in terms of employment and rise in income levels, it has also had some negative impact. The introduction of cash economy has led to radical changes. The villages which were self-sufficient in economy, have now to depend on the market for most of their requirements. The people show an increased tendency to purchase fashionable items and spend most of their compensation money on clothes, cosmetics and liquor. Their earnings and purchasing capacity have increased no doubt, but their wants are also multiplied. The use of materialistic items had necessitated extra income. The uprooted people have been paid compensation in cash for their lossess of property, but being mostly illiterate and not materialistic in values, they could not utilise the money in proper way. The amount has been largely spent on repaying old debts, purchasing fashionable articles, food items and consumption of liquor. Only a little amount has been utilised in acquiring lands or depositing in banks (Reddy, 1983).

Although the government has promised to provide employment to at least one person from each displaced family, it has not been possible to provide jobs to everyone, because the plant is based on latest technology, which requires little manpower in the project. Further, what is one family at the time of the commencement of the project, may become more families over the years, as the nuclear family is the norm among the tribes and sons establish separate homes as soon as they are married. Thus, non-provision of employment to all adult male members may lead to frustration among the uprooted people. For instance, the deprivation of a job in the project of one of the displaced led to the killing of an Additional District Magistrate. Further, the project officials have expressed that during the initial stages, working in the project was always risky because there was a threat of being attacked by the frustrated tribal youth, who are deprived of employment (*The Hindu*, 1988).

The uprooted people were paid very low rates of compensation for their lands. The compensation paid to them varied between Rs. 1500 to Rs. 4500 for various types of lands, (cf. Table-3) ; the prevailing market value of lands were reported to be Rs. 1000 to Rs. 8000 (Reddy, 1983).

The land cost was determined on the basis of registered sale deeds of lands in the project area. The uprooted people alleged that the method of determining the land values was not justified because the buyers usually record a lower amount in the registered sale deeds in order to avoid the payment of stamp duty. As a result they were paid compensation at a lower rate and were consequently unable to purchase alternative lands of similar type and quantum due to the high market prices.

TABLE 3

Compensation paid and prevailing Market Value for various types of land

(Amount in Rs. per acre)

Type of land*	Compensation paid (a) (Rs)	Estimated market value (b) (Rs)
Paddy I	4344	8000—10000
Paddy II	3900	5500— 8000
Paddy III	3571	4000— 6000
Donger I	2500	2000— 2500
Donger II	1973	1500— 2000
Donger III	1550	1000— 1800

*The type of land is classified by the Assistant Settlement Officer on the basis of : i) crop or crops grown on the land ; ii) nature of soil ; iii) situation of the land ; and iv) source of irrigation.

Source : (a) NALCO Project Office, Damarjodi

(b) Information based on respondents' views during the survey, 1983

Impact on Social System

The execution of large industrial projects in backward tribal areas solves the purpose of modifications in the cultural patterns along with development in economic techniques. Thus economic development is sure to materialise with changes in old social values and traditional organisations of rural societies. The continuous interaction of uprooted as well as local people with outsiders belonging to different communities has broadened the views of local people and thus helped them to get rid of superstitions, beliefs and age-old customs to a great extent. The women in the project area are fast becoming changed to modernity. Further, the economic and social independence coupled with modernisation have also conditioned several changes among women folk. There is also greater spread of education among local people and are becoming more conscious about the public health and started using modern medicines.

Besides having certain positive social impact on the uprooted people, the project has had some negative social ramifications. The greatest adverse impact is the displacement of tribals from their ancestral habitat and loss of traditional occupations like agriculture, forestry and associated activities. The eviction of tribals from their habitat is the most serious aspect of displacement. Forests and the natural surroundings play an important role in the social and cultural life of tribals. These natural surroundings are not provided for in the new settlements. Although the government has paid compensation, it did not help in counterbalancing the social and psychological disturbances. It is also noticed that a new class of contractors has developed in the project area. There is a sporadic increase in the incidence of crime and other illegal activities including forcing liquor and other vices on innocent people.

The tribal societies which were once close and integrated are now becoming loose. The people have become more materialistic and individualistic. Inter-personal relationships which were based on kinship ties and sense of familiarity have become more impersonal and indifferent. Mutual help and cooperation for each other at the time of need has completely disappeared in the new resettlement colonies. In the process they have lost their homogeneity, which is a tribal characteristic. Tobacco, *ganja* and *bhang* are also consumed in large quantities. Instead of native rice beer, distilled liquor which is harmful and more intoxicating has become popular. Further, the breaking up of village organisation and corporate life along with acquiring many habits like exces drinking, use of cosmetics, costly clothes, *etc.* have also drained away most of their resources.

Environmental Hazards

The establishment of large industries has brought certain environmental hazards, which will ultimately affect man, animal and plants. The NALCO project is no exception to these environmental ramifications. Emission of pollutants in the air, release of effluents in water, and dumping of solid wastes in the open is bound to cause many a health hazard. The major environmental problems associated with the project are : (1) disturbance of the land itself ; (2) soil erosion ; (3) mine run-off ; (4) dislocation of water balance ; (5) generation of dust, noise and fumes ; (6) spread of diseases and disturbances of natural economic systems; and (7) disturbances caused by the creation of infrastructure. Further, it is estimated that the open cast mining can generate 0.25 kg. of dust per metric tonne of bauxite mining during digging, stock filling, loading and dyeing operations. In addition significant air pollution from exhaust fumes during heavy vehicular movement and noise pollution will collude in spreading the diseases to man, animal and crops (Sreenivasan, *et. al.* 1981).

CONCLUSION

Though the NALCO project has induced substantial benefits in the form of creating additional employment and improvement of various infrastructure amenities, the damages are outstripping the benefits as most of the benefits are accruing to the unaffected community rather than to the uprooted people. Due to lack of enough skills among the uprooted, the skilled jobs in the project are mostly secured by the outsiders, thus reducing the uprooted people to casual labour. Though the project created a greater demand for various agricultural products, the benefits again have gone to the unaffected community, because the uprooted people have lost their agricultural land and due to low compensation rates they could not purchase alternative agricultural land.

The uprooted people require a planned approach of rehabilitation to minimise the hardships as these traditional people show a great attachment to their habitat, land and other belonging which are so near and dear to them for generation of the uprooted people in industrial project includes :

(1) The tribals and other backward people have a strong attachment to their soil. Therefore every effort should be made to select the resettlement site in accordance with the liking of the uprooted people. This would help in preserving their own way of life and also winning their confidence. Efforts should be made to involve the leaders of affected people in the process of planning and execution of rehabilitation measures in order

to take the oustee into confidence and for proper adjustment in the new environment ;

(2) The compensation amount should not be paid fully in cash to prevent misuti isation. Instead alternative arrangements should be made for acquiring permanent assets. Further, provisions should be made for paying an *ex-gratia* amount to those families who do not have any lands and assets, to meet expenses during the transitional period ;

(3) One of the important aspects of rehabilitation is to provide an alternative gainful employment to the uprooted people. Therefore, various training programmes suitable for tribal aptitudes should be started to enhance the skills among the uprooted, so that they can eventually be absorbed in the projects ;

(4) All government sponsored employment programmes should be made available to the uprooted and appropriate safeguards should be evolved in agreement with the contractors of various works and the project authorities for providing employment opportunities on a continuous basis ;

(5) Since there is a wide scope for self-employment, it is also necessary to train them in managerial functions, which is very important for self-employed entrepreneurs. In addition, organising and financing for gainful vocations like poultry, farming, animal husbandry, cottage industries, fishery, kitchen gardening, *etc.* should go a long way in improving the living standards of the uprooted as well as the local people. Further, they should be encouraged to adopt a production pattern based on actudneeds of the people in town ships for improving their earning capacities.

(6) Proper attention should be given to the environmental protection and necessary steps should be taken for maintaining the ecological balance in the project area ; and

(7) Lastly, the integrated development of the region should be planned in such a way as to achieve a balance between technological and cultural development,

between agricultural and industrial economy, between rural and urban industrial way of life. These changes must be brought gradually and continuously along with their traditional institutions to enable them for adjusting to the changed ceonomy and society as well as promoting a more heterogeneous socio-economic development.

The various guidelines put forward in this paper are of prime importance for planned rehabilitation of the uprooted people. The very objective of establishing large industrial projects for the development of backward tribal areas will be achieved only when the uprooted people are properly resettled, otherwise the very cause of development through industrialisation will be lost.

REFERENCES

DAS, J.C., Walter Fernandes and Sam Rao, (1988) "The Extent and Prospects of Displacement", *Social Action*.

MUTHAYYA, B.C., Tripathy, R.N., Santhanam, M.L. and Srivastava, O.N., (1984). *Rehabilitation of Displaced Villagers : A Plan*, Hyderabad : National Institute of Rural Development.

REDDY, I.U.B., (1983) *Social and Economic Rehabilitation of People affected by NALCO-Upper Kolab Projects*, M.R.P. Dissertation (unpublished), Kharagpur, Indian Institute of Technology.

REDDY, I.U.B. and Chattopadhyay, R.N. (1987), "NALCO Project : Need for Manpower Development", *Small Enterprises Development, Management and Extension Journal*, 14(2), pp. 1-8.

REDDY, N.S., (1989). "Development, Displacement and Resettlement", Keynote Address National Seminar on "*Developmental Process and the Problems of Rehabilitation and Relocation of the Uprooted*", 13-14 March 1989, University of Madras.

SREENIVASAN, G., (1987). "National Income Looks up in 1985-86", *Yojana*, 31 (5), pp. 10-11.

SREENIVASAN, K., Vinod Vyasulu and Rajagopalan, S. (1981). "The Orissa Aluminium Complex : Points toward a Debate", *Economic and Political Weekly*. 16 (49), pp. 2005-2015.

THE HINDU, (1988). "Incurable Birth Pangs of a National Project", 7 October.

VIDYARTHI, L P. (1970). *Social-Cultural Implications of Industrialisation in India ; A Case Study of Tribal Bihar*, New Delhi, Research Programme Committee, Planning Commission, Government of India.

8

Role of Enumeration in the Rehabilitation of the Displaced Due to Visakha Steel Project

R. Yathiraj Kumar*

Development programmes may not result in positive changes for all. 'Displacement' is one example of the negative consequences of developmental programmes. Thousands of families have been displaced from their age-old habitat and way of life, in different parts of our country since Independence, due to the establishment of heavy industries, defence projects, construction of major irrigation and hydro-electric projects, *etc.* under programmes of planned development and change. Their case is one of forced migration.

Rehabilitation measures follow displacement which aim at, ideally, to resettle the affected populations and ensure continuity of life patterns. But the findings of various social scientists point out that in many a case, the rehabilitation measures are 'mechanical' and 'inadequate'; exposing the affected popula-

*Department of Anthropology, Andhra University, Waltair.

tion to deep-rooted changes in life patterns and prolonged suffering. All along, the affected populations, mostly rural and tribal, were observed to bear with the situation stoically due to their intrinsic inadequacies, *viz.* poor literacy levels, ignorance of bureaucratic procedures, submission to authority, gullibility, *etc.* However, in recent times organized resistance against establishment of large projects is gaining ground, drawing from the distressing experiences of the displaced in earlier situations. The ongoing movements in Orissa against the establishment of Missile Range at Baliapal, Sardar Sarovar and Indira Sagar Dams in M.P., Pulichintala Irrigation Project in Andhra Pradesh are cases in point. The situation needs a thorough analysis.

The studies (Dhebar, 1960 ; Dubey, 1967 ; Sinha, 1967 ; Karve, 1969 ; Tandon, 1970 ; Muthayya and Mathur, 1975 ; Naidu, 1977 ; Korsching *et. al.*, 1980 ; Das Gupta, 1981 ; Reddy and Chattopadhay, 1986) in the field of 'displacement and rehabilitation' in our country so far have concentrated more on the socio-economic and cultural impact due to displacement and inadequacies of rehabilitation measures and related areas. Relatively less importance was bestowed on the aspect of 'enumeration' which has great significance and the foremost step in any displacement and rehabilitation situation.

Enumeration means counting or listing of things. It involves the complete and comprehensive recording of displaced persons and their fixed assets. The fixation and payment of compensation, allotment of alternate lands, house-site, housing loan, alternative and preferential employment opportunities, subsidies and other privileges for the displaced under rehabilitation measures, depend on the data based on enumeration. In short, the future of displaced depends on the quality of enumeration. This paper aims at understanding the process on the displaced in a concrete displacement situation—among the displaced due to the construction of a massive Steel Plant at Visakhapatnam.

The Visakha Steel Project (VSP)

It is officially known as Rashtriya Ispat Nigam Limited (RINL). The total cost, according to the latest (28-2-1989) estimates is around Rs. 7,000 crores with an annual steel output of 3.5 million tonnes and is expected to be completed by March, 1991. The establishment of VSP necessitated the acquisition of 26,710.65 acres of land, of which 57% is private land, displacing 14,000 families belonging to 57 villages. In the first phase of displacement, 1,400 families exclusively belonging to four fishermen villages are resettled at Dibbapalaem rehabilitation colony on a 103.50 acre plot and another 4,418 families of 24 displaced agricultural villages are resettled at Pedagantyada Rehabilitation Colony spread over an 451.75 acre plot. In the second phase of displacement, the remaining displaced families of 29 villages are being resettled at five rehabilitation colonies.

Methodology

The study has been conducted in the two rehabilitation colonies (RC's) established under the first phase. Two villages in each RC are randomly selected. The sample comprises 294 households randomly selected from the four selected villages constituting 38.58% of the total households in these villages. It should be noted that the settlement pattern in the RC's maintains the village identity at the time of displacement. Schedule, interview-guide, observation, field-diary are the main tools employed. Secondary data was gathered from various official sources.

An outline of the Enumeration Process

The survey of the land to be acquired for the VSP commenced in 1969. The foundation stone was laid in 1971 and Project feasibility report was prepared. But from 1971-79, periodic spurts of activity and uncertainty marked the progress of steel plant work. Serious work commenced only in 1979, after signing an agreement on 12-1-1979 with the Soviet Union ensuring financial and technical collaboration.

The enumeration of the displaced households and their assets commenced in 1971. A special officer (Steel Plant) was appointed by the State Government to coordinate the activities of Land Acquisition, Enumeration of households, property, fixation and payment of compensation and other rehabilitation measures. He was assisted by the revenue department officials such as Deputy Collectors, Tahsildars, Revenue Inspectors,

Village Munsiffs and Karanams. The services of Engineering Department staff are drawn on deputation to assist and assess the value of fixed property such as dwellings and other structure and also to plan and execute the civil works related to the establishment of Rehabilitation Colonies. None of them had any specialized training or orientation for the task.

After the completion of enumeration, a Rehabilitation Card popularly known as 'R' card is prepared for each displaced family containing the particulars of the head and members of the family, their assets, socio-economic background, *etc.* 'R' card has great significance in the lives of the displaced because it establishes the identity and displaced status and serves as a passport enabling them to receive all the benefits and privilages under rehabilitation measures.

Results and Discussion

The data gathered reveal that enumeration was taken up without proper and advanced notice to the displaced ; many outsiders managed to get enumerated as displaced and cornered most of the benefits of rehabilitation to the great disadvantage of the genuinely displaced; corruption, nepotism and adhocism marked the enumeration ; compensation fixation was arbitrary ; leadership marked by the change of role traditional village elite into 'middlemen', *etc.* causing distress to the displaced on many fronts. The following discussion throws light on these aspects.

Communication Gap

Displacement being a frustrating experience has both material and psychological connotations and warrants delicate handling. Advanced communication about the impending event and procedure of enumeration shall facilitate the people involved to prepare for the situation. Data from Table-1 reveal that most of the information channels are informal or through observation after the enumeration has actually commenced. None had advanced official information.

Enumeration Criteria : The Lapses

Initially (between 1971-79), the absentee landlords with agricultural land or house-sites located in the land acquired

TABLE 1

Sources of First Information About Displacement

Sl. No.	Source of Information	DPRC No. of responses	DPRC % N=178	PGRC No. of responses	PGRC % N=118	TOTAL No. of responses	TOTAL % N=294
1.	Village elite and neighbours	119	67.61	72	61.01	197	64.96
2.	Acquisition notices	18	10.23	21	17.79	39	13.26
3.	Land Survey Operations	3	1.70	11	9.32	14	4.76
4.	When palm prints were	2	1.14	—	—	22	0.68
5.	When houses were demolished	3	1.73	—	—	3	1.02
6.	Foundation laying ceremony by Mrs. Gandhi	31	17.61	14	11.86	45	15.31
	TOTAL	176	99.99	118	99.98	294	99.99

for VSP expected that they shall come under displaced category and entertained high expectations of the privileges and benefits to be drawn, more importantly employment in steel plant. But it was officially clarified in 1979 that "only those who lost their houses in the village sites acquired for the steel plant and actually living in the villages before 1974 are only eligible for displaced status".* Similarly, there was confusion on whether to record displaced status at the household level (a residential unit with extended families) or at individual nuclear family level. It was clarified by the same committee that in case of extended families only the individual families of father, major married brother or son, widowed sister-in-law or daughter-in-law, if they are not remarried, should be accorded displaced status individually.

The lack of clarity on these issues of enumeration till 1979 facilitated many 'outsiders' (absentee landlords, land speculators, kith and kin of some influential persons and some of the enterprising among the displaced, to resort to other means to get displaced status and acquire an 'R' card. Their *modus operandi* is as follows : They got their bonafides established as the residents of the displaced villages by erecting temporary thatched sheds, getting them assessed for house-tax by the village panchayat from a back-date and clearing the same, aequiring a ration card, *etc*. The village officials, *viz.* munsiff, karnam and sarpanch, empowered to certify the bonafides of a resident helped these, for a consideration. The enumeration staff, it was revealed, recorded these particulars without proper verification, thus conniving with village officials and thereby helped the outsiders.

Similarly some of the influential village elite in the displaced villages got each household enumerated into a number of independent units. It was alleged that a room, a verandah got enumerated as a separate household. An investigative news report in a Telugu local daily reveals the intensity of the problem. "In Kanithi village, a small hut which can hardly accommodate 15 people in sitting posture is shown as con-

*At a meeting of the high level committee held at Hyderabad on September 1, 1979 headed by the Chief Secretary, Government of Andhra Pradesh.

sisting of the independent portions occupied by separate households. Each of these ten housholds were shown to have on an average three major sons. Thus a single thatched shed which would have got one R-card, has now got enumerated as 30 displaced households and got 30 'R' cards" (*Enadu*, March 5, 1986).

Also it was gathered that there was sale and transfer of 'R' cards from genuine displaced to outsiders. This was possible because of the official provision that old, infirm and childless can nominate a heir, which was skilfully exploited by outsiders. Some among the displaced households which got or managed to get more than one 'R' card, sold the extra ones at substantial price to outsiders. According to Appanna (pseudonym) of Musalanaidupalem "I am very old (60 years) and my only son has died long ago. I am unfit for any employment in Steel Plant. I can live anywhere. Why should I refuse the money offered for my 'R' card ? It shall be useful in this old age. Anyhow I cannot work. It is problematic even to get on every day." These irregularities are reported to have been committed at all levels during enumeration, especially between 1971-79, as there was no proper monitoring and checks. As a result, the number of displaced households got more than doubled from the originally estimated six thousand households to 14,000 by early 1980s, to the great disadvantage of the genuine displaced and also placing additional burden on the State. The fact that the Special Officer (Steel Plant) advertised in the local press in 1984-85 seeking information from all concerned about the bogus Rehabilitation Cards and also the fact that 370 bogus 'R' cards have been cancelled by the end of 1985 confirms the situation. Many more cases are under investigation.

Data on Table-2 indicates that a significant number of respondents (34%) had some problem or other in getting an 'R' card, which include 10.88% whose kin are left out during enumeration. Payment of bribes to officials and middlemen to get an 'R' card was mentioned by 21.08% of the respondents, ranging from Rs. 100 to Rs. 4,000 (Table-3).

TABLE 2

Problems Faced in Getting the 'R'CARD

Sl. No.	Nature of problem	No. of responses	% N—294
1.	Paid bribes to get his own R-Card	16	5.44
2.	Paid bribes to get the 'R' Cards for his son(s)	27	9.18
3.	Brother(s)	4	1.36
4.	Brother-in-law	1	0.34
5.	Paid commission/expenses to middlemen	14	4.76
6.	Forced to go round the offices a number of times	37	12.59
7.	No problem	192	65.31
8.	Others	3	1.02
	TOTAL	294	100.00

TABLE 3

Amounts Paid as Bribes to get 'R' Card

Amount paid as bribe (Rs.)	No. of responses	% N—62
100—500	21	33.87
501—1000	12	79.35
1001—1500	6	9.68
1501—2000	13	20.97
2001—2500	3	4.84
2501—3000	3	4.84
3001—3500	1	1.61
3501—4000	3	4.84
4001 and above	—	—
TOTAL	62	100.00

Enumeration of Fixed Property

Land holdings, dwellings, farm houses, cattle sheds, household and irrigation wells, house-sites, trees, orchards, constituted fixed property and were enumerated, classified and their value was assessed by revenue staff assisted by engineering staff, as per the guidelines presented in the Annexure.

In determining the qualitative aspects of the type of construction, age of the structure, measurements of the plinth area of buildings, diametre and depth of wells, the final decision is made by the engineering staff. Similarly, the revenue officials are empowered with determining the extent of land holdings, productivity classification of land, number of trees, orchards, house-sites, and their measurements. This is one significant area, where there is scope for subjectivity and arbitrariness. The respondents alleged that during this phase, over or under valuation of property has taken place in many instances.

It could be observed from Table-4 that 82.52% of respondents had some problem or other with regard to enumeration and valuation of property. These include 44.56% of respondents whose responses reflect the apathy and helplessness ; 17.69% of the respondents were dissatisfied and who applied for revision of valuation. Land survey (measurement of individual land-holdings) was another major source of dissatisfaction.

Though the Revenue Survey officials claim that prior notice was given about the time and date of land measurements in displaced villages, respondents allege that the information has not reached many and as such they were away during land measurements. It was also informed that in other cases, the survey officials have not turned up at the appointed time and carried on land measurements at their convenience when the owners were absent. It was informed that, in many a case, ordinary villagers cultivate the land within the contours of 'Gatlu' (bunds) by blind practice and are not aware of the actual measurements and depended upon *munsiffs* and *karnams*. It was complained that the ignorance of such villagers was exploited by land survey officials with the connivance of *munsiffs* and *karnams*. The following case-study reflect the situation.

"A.N. is a resident of Musilinaidupalem and 52 years old. He was paying land tax for five acres of dry land for long.

TABLE 4

Attitudes and Opinions on the Valuation of Fixed Property and Compensation Paid

Sl. No.	Nature of the Problem	DPRC		PGRC		TOTAL	
		No. of responses	% N=176	No. of responses	% N=118	No. of responses	% N=294
1.	No problem	14	7.95	8	6.78	22	7.43
2.	No say for us	55	31.25	27	22,88	82	27.89
3.	Accepted what the Government has offered	34	19.32	15	12.71	49	16.67
4.	Compensation amount was known only when received the money	19	10.80	9	7.63	28	9.52
5.	Not satisfied, applied for revision	21	11.93	31	26.27	52	17.69
6.	Informed of the land survey, but the officials have not turned up	—	—	5	4.24	5	1.70

7.	Though I know about land survey I could not be present as I went for work	2	1.18	5	4.24	7	2.38
8.	I was not in the village at the time of land survey	—	—	9	7.63	9	3.06
9.	Nobody informed about the land survey	4	2.27	7	5.93	11	3.74
10.	Don't know	27	15.34	2	1.69	29	9.86
	TOTAL	176	100.00	118	100.00	294	99.99

At the time of land survey he was away working in the salt mines. He was informed later by the revenue officials that his land measurement came to three acres. He had no option but to accept it. His complaint to the officials had no effect. He complained that the bunds around his land were not taken into consideration d ring survey. These bunds have many palmyrah trees. Thus, he lost compensation for both land and palmyrah trees."

In a few cases, the local village factions appear to have played their role. Opponents of the village officials and elite (assisting the enumeration staff) were put hardship where as their faction members were unduly favoured.

Valuation of Houses

The respondents informed that in many cases they got much less compensation for their evacuated houses, than the then prevailing market value. The estimation by respondents of the market value of their houses appears to be reasonable and moderate as can be seen from Table-5. It was complained that influential persons got more than what they are eligible for while the poor and uninformed got a raw deal.

TABLE 5

Perceived Approximate Value And the Actual Compensation Received for Evacuated Houses

	Market value of the evacuated house as perceived by the Respondents		Actual Compensation received	
	N=294	%	N=294	=
Below—1000	0	—	30	10.20
1,000— 2,500	81	27.55	115	40.48
2,501— 5,000	88	29.93	84	28.57
5,001—10,000	81	27.55	41	13.95
10,002—10,000	29	9.86	8	2.72
15,001—20,000	9	3.06	5	1.70
20,001—25,000	3	1.02	4	1.36
25,001 and above	3	1.02	3	1,02
TOTAL	294	99.99	294	100.00

Conclusion

The above discussion points out that the enumeration process has commenced without clear guidelines and continued for nearly eight years, giving scope for confusion and corruption, facilitating many outsiders to get displaced status. The escalation in the number of displaced families has not only affected the prospects of the genuine displaced but also placed additional burden on the State. The enumeration process has also facilitated the vocal, worldly village elite turn into middlemen. The scope for subjectivity in valuation of fixed assets, in the absence of proper monitoring and cross-checks, handled by personnel with a mechanical, authoritative approach, lead to over or under-valuation of property. As a consequence, perceptible differences are observed to have resulted between the expected market value and the official assessment, often leading to frustration among the displaced. The situation also points out at the need to involve an average displaced person in the process, the need to take his views and educate him wherever necessary on the procedural aspects.

Sound planning, clear guidelines, mechanisms for cross-check and monitoring, involvement of voluntary agencies and social scientists, a more adaptive and responsive rehabilitation administration shall help to overcome these problems and make the enumeration more thorough and scientific, thereby mitigating the sufferings of an average displaced, uprooted from his traditional moorings.

REFERENCES

HOROBIN, G.W. (1957) "Adjustment and Assimilation : The Displaced Person", *Sociological Review*, Vol. V, pp. 239-54.

DHEBAR, M.N. (1960) *Report on Uprooted Tribals of Central India* (New Delhi : Planning Commission).

DUBEY S.M. (1967) "Displacement, Mobility and Conformity with Outgroup" *Interdiscipline* Vol. 4(2).

SINHA, D.P. (1967) "Socio-Cultural Implications of Economic Development in Banari : The Case of Birhor Resettlement" *The Eastern Anthropologist*, Vol, XX, No. 2.

KARVE, IRAVATHI (1969) A Survey of the People Displaced through Koyana Dam, Poona, Deccan College.

MUTHAYYA, B.C., &MATHUR, J.S. (1975) *Rehabilitation of Displaced Villagers : A Socio-Economic and Attitudinal Study in an Agro-Industrial Complex in Rural Andhra Pradesh* (Hyderabad : National Institute of Community Development).

NAIDU, N.Y. (1977) "The displaced Villagers and their Problem", *Folklore*, 54, Feb. 1977.

ANNEXURE

Guidelines Followed for Enumeration of Fixed Property

Cultivable dry land/ac.	:	Rs. 1050—Rs. 1270/-
Cultivable wet land/ac.	:	Rs. 1500—Rs. 2500/-
House-sites/Sq. yard	:	Rs. 2.70 —Rs. 4.00

Dwellings;

Type	Average Life*	Acquisition of plinth area/sq. ft.
Thatched	20 years	Rs. 10—12/-
T iled house	40 years	Rs. 35—40/-
Terraced houses:		
R.C.C. houses	75 years	Rs. 80—100/-
Madras Terrace	70 years	Rs. 80—100/-
Wells (household or Agricultural)	55 years	Rs. 3,000—10,000/-

*Depreciation is calculated as per the age of the house under enumeration.

Trees

Palmyrah (thati chettu)	Rs. 3—12/-
Wild-date tree (Eetha chettu)	Rs. 2—4/-
Tamarind	Rs. 24/-
Coconut (yielding or non-yielding)	Rs. 5/- 25/-
All other trees	Rs. 18/- cart load of wood

Source : Office of the Special Officer (Steel Plant), Visakhapatnam.

SHARMA, B.D. (1977) "Industrial Complexes and their Tribal Hinterlands ; A Conceptual Frame of their Problems and Prospects ', *Eastern Anthropologist*, Vol. 30, No. 1, Lucknow.

KORSCHING PETER, F., JOSEPH, N., DONNERMEYER, and RABEL J. BURDGE (1980) "Perception of Property Settlement Payments and Replacement Housing among Displaced Persons," *Human Organisation*, Vol. 39, No. 4. pp. 332-338.

DAS GUPTA, P.K. (1981) "Tribes in the Industrial Context of India", *Man and Life*, Vol. 7, Nos. 3 & 4, Calcutta.

REDDY, I.U.B., & CHATTOPADHYAY, R.N. (1986) "Impact of Large Projects on Displaced Persons : A Case Study", *Eastern Anthropologist* Vol. 39, No. 2.

KUMAR, R.Y. (1988) "A Report on Displacement and Rehabilitation : A Study of the Displaced due to Visakha Steel Project with special reference to Women and Children", New Delhi : Ministry of Welfare.

SECTION III

Rehabilitation : A Policy Perspective

9

A Framework for Planned Rehabilitation

Dr. B.L. Joshi*

This paper is based on my research work carried out prior to the displacement and rehabilitation in one of the dam-affected village communities situated in the reservoir belt of the Jayakwadi (Godawari) Irrigation Project near Paithan in Aurangabad district of Maharashtra State.

Displacement of people due to construction of dams is a world-wide phenomenon. Displacement of people may also occur due to various circumstances such as wars, racial and religious persecutions, repatriation of the alien minorities and natural calamities like earthquakes, floods, great fires and famines. The rehabilitation of people displaced as a result of the construction of dams and other developmental activities is quite different from the process arising from political and natural calamities. The political and natural calamities are solved mostly by undertaking hurried temporary

*Reader in Sociology, Marathwada University, Aurangabad (Maharashtra).

relief work before steps for permanent rehabilitation are taken. But rehabilitation arising from the construction of dams entails a calculated, well thought-out pre-planned programme.

I give below a scheme for planned rehabilitation. It may be useful to the planners and executors of rehabilitation work in particular and to others in general.

The process of rehabilitation from the stage of acquisition of immovable properties—land and houses—and actual moving and rehabilitation to the problems after rehabilitation of the affected people requires a planned approach. The planned approach may minimise the hardships of the affected people and they can be rehabilitated smoothly. This is necessary in view of the fact that they are uprooted from the home and hearth to which they show deep attachments, from their socio-economic life in which they are traditionally rooted. The economic compensation may not satisfactorily counterbalance the social and psychological disturbances. They need to be rehabilitated not only economically but socially and psychologically as well. This requires the planners and executors of the scheme of rehabilitation to draw and implement the scheme foresightedly so that the hardships coming in the way of the affected people would be minimised and that they may not have to repent after their rehabilitation.

A Plan of Rehabilitation

After the acquisition of land and houses, the compensation should not be paid to the owners of land and houses. The Government should deposit the compensation of the respective affected owners of land and houses in the bank. From the date of acquisition of land and houses to the actual depositing of compensation money in the bank, the affected people will get interest at the bank rate on the quantum of compensation fixed from the Government. After depositing amounts in the bank, the bank will continue to pay interest in the regular course.

If the affected ex-land owners have to purchase land they will submit proposals to the Government, giving particulars of land, name of the owners of land and the value of the land to be purchased. The Government will scrutinise the proposals and allow the people to purchase new land and will arrange to pay the value of the land directly to the land owners who are to sell their land.

There may be some difficulties inherent in this process. It will increase the work of the Government. The affected land owners may not be ready to accept such proposals. But since the Government have to look after the rehabilitation work of the affected people, it may not be very difficult to mould public opinion in this direction. As soon as the people get compensation, they go on spending it as they like. This then creates problems for the people. The people rely on assistance from the Government and agitate for help in some way or the other. The Government has also to consider some requests of the people. If this is to be stopped, it becomes necessary to take steps in such a way that the affected people will be rehabilitated in their own compensation money.

Likewise, only after the allotment of sites for rehabilitation the compensation money should be released to the people to enable them to construct houses. For the poorer people, a scheme should be drawn and implemented for giving them small readymade houses at the site of rehabilitation. Their compensation be utilised for this purpose.

The point to be considered here is that the land owners are allowed to cultivate their acquired holdings till final submergence and they are allowed to reside in the acquired houses till they are rehabilitated elsewhere. Hence the people need not clamour for compensation money when there are no plans of rehabilitation in view. In the circumstances, it is proper to arouse public opinion in the submerged area in favour of utilisation of money for rehabilitation only, and to ensure that the Government holds their compensation temporarily, and will see that the same is utilised properly. There may be some unrest among the people over this matter for the time being, but ultimately it would be beneficial both to the people as well as to the Government.

The policy of the Government is that there will be rehabilitation of the affected people first and then the construction work of the irrigation project will be undertaken. But practically it is seen that the construction work of the irrigation project gains momentum and the rehabilitation work moves slowly. This results in the completion of the irrigation project earlier than the rehabilitation work. This completion of the project then forces the people to shift early to the new site of rehabilitation to avoid damages to their lives and properties or belongings. Those people whose houses are not ready by that time, are compulsorily shifted to the new site of rehabilitation. The illiterate masses have not experienced such uncommon situation. Secondly, the greater reliance on the Government makes them least worried of the future. Such a situation results in unplanned rehabilitation. The Government is required to gear its machinery to remedy the things as far as possible. It is uncertain that all the problems would be solved.

So far I have given at length the scheme of utilization of compensation money. I give below a scheme of rehabilitation which is based on my understanding of the problems of displacement and rehabilitation of the affected people and my own interpretation of the situation.

After the declaration of the construction work of the irrigation project, steps are taken to acquire land and houses. Simultaneously the work of acquisition of land from the proposed command area should be undertaken. The people of the submerged area are allowed to cultivate their acquired holdings. The plan of allotment of land from the command area be kept ready and made known to the people well in advance. The new site of rehabilitation be selected and allotted to the people immediately. The land to be allotted to the people from the command area be as far as possible in the vicinity of the place of rehabilitation or the place of rehabilitation be selected and allotted to the project affected people where land is available. Those land owners who would get land at a longer distance be rehabiliatted in the villages near the land. As soon as the people are rehabilitated, the land acquired from the command area be given to them. The cost of such land should be deducted directly from their compensation. As far as possible, the people may be rehabilitated in the command area of the irrigation project.

Civic Amenities

All the civic amenities are not provided at the site of rehabilitation. As soon as the site for rehabilitation is allotted, the machinery should be geared to provide civic amenities there without waiting for the demands to come from the people. A plan of civic amenities to be provided to each affected village be prepared, made known to the people, budget provision be made and the plan be implemented without any delay. This would help in rehabilitating the people smoothly.

Creation of high power Autonomous Body for Rehabilitation Work

The rehabilitation of the affected people is as important as the construction work of the irrigation project. Many problems crop up during the process of rehabilitation and even after rehabilitation. Much time is also spent in solving the unforeseen problems and it results in delay in executing the rehabilitation plan. Different agencies are engaged in the rehabilitation work ; likewise, different agencies are engaged in the construction of irrigation project. If efficient and prompt coordination is not sought among the agencies engaged in rehabilitation work themselves and the construction of irrigation project, the new problems that crop up during the process of execution or after execution of rehabilitation work would not be solved promptly. To achieve better results in the work of rehabilitation, it is imperative that there should be efficient coordination and prompt action among different agencies. It is, therefore, suggested that an autonomous body be created on the lines of the agency such as the 'Command Area Development Authority' which, while drawing and implementing schemes of development of the command area coordinates the work among different agencies like agriculture, irrigation, cooperation, *etc.* This autonomous body will have sufficient power and finance to solve all the problems of rehabilitation at its own level.

The quantum of land acquired from the command area for allotment to the affected people may not be sufficient to meet the demands of all the affected land owners. They get bits of land in proportion to the land owned by them prior to rehabilitation. Many problems arise in this respect. Sometimes the allotted land in some cases is taken up for actual cultivation much later. It is noticed that the ex-land owners do not willingly allow the affected land owners to cultivate their allotted land. Sometimes the distance between the land allotted and the place of rehabilitation is great. It becomes difficult to foot the distance everyday for agricultural operations. Some affected land owners purchase new land at one place. They get land from the command area at another place. Such land owners find it difficult to cultivate both the pieces of land simultaneously. It is feared that such a situation may give way to absentee landlordism in future. This should be avoided. Those ex-land owners who will not get land from the command area for cultivation should be rehabilitated occupationally.

The ex-owners of small holdings, agricultural labourers and artisans may be given facility of earning an income from non-agricultural sources. The survival of these sections of people depends upon the survival of land owners. If the land owners do not purchase land equal to their acquired holdings or get land from the command area, these people will have no stake in the agricultural pursuit. For the people of these categories, the following scheme may be drawn and implemented.

(1) To provide employment to unskilled, semi-skilled and skilled persons on priority basis.

(3) To institute technical courses for training the affected people and/or their dependents. For this purpose, special training courses through Industrial Training Institutes be run in the vicinity of the rehabilitated villages. For this, a unit of 15 to 20 or if it becomes a bigger unit, a unit of 10 to 15 villages be brought under one Industrial Training Institute which will run the courses as detailed below :

I. House Mechanic Courses :
1. Brick-making,
2. Masonry,
3. Plumbing,
4. Pipe fitting.

II.	Structural Mechanic Courses :	1. Welding, 2. Painting.
III.	Workshop Courses : 1. Auto Mechanic :	1. Tractor, Oil engine repairs, 2. Turner 3. Fitter 4. Electrician 5. Lathe Operator
IV.	Wood Work	1. Furniture making and fittings 2. Wood work machine operating 3. Carpentry
V.	Leather Work :	Shoe-making and leather work
VI.	Pottery Work :	Making of earthen-wares
VII.	Smithy work.	

The other courses suitable to the rural people may also be introduced.

The project affected people and their dependents may be recruited as per their aptitude and choice to these training courses. To facilitate them to undergo training, a suitable stipend be given to them.

The Government should give instructions to the respective Employment Exchanges falling within the jurisdiction of the rehabilitated villages to give priority to these trained affected people for employment. Or an independent placement machinery be set up to contact the different agencies of public and private sectors and place these trained people into them.

If some of the affected trained people do not want placement in employment and if they are ready to run small workshop, small industries, petty trades, auto service, *etc.* they may be given loans on long term repayment basis charging nominal interest on the loans advanced.

The State Government encourages the decentralised industrial growth around cities and towns in the State. This work is entrusted to the State Industrial Development Corporation. This Corporation may look to the possibility in consultation with the special autonomous authority of establishing industrial estates in the vicinity of the rehabilitated villages. The trainees that may come out from the Industrial Training Institutes as said earlier may be encouraged by giving them financial assistance to run their own small industries, workshops, trades, *etc.* on individual basis or on cooperative basis by forming cooperative societies. Simultaneously, the other outside entrepreneur may also be encouraged and attracted to run their industries here as per the usual scheme of the Corporation. This may provide job opportunities to the affected people.

The alternate plan of rehabilitation of the affected villages is suggested below. It may be seen how far this plan can be brought into practice.

Scheme of Model Small Towns

A scheme of developing model small towns at the central places in the project affected area be drawn and implemented.

The work of establishing model towns or cities or twin cities is undertaken at present in Maharashtra State through the City and Industrial Development Corporation (CIDCO). The twin cities are meant to lessen the burden of the already existing cities. The CIDCO machinery may be utilised in a better way for establishing small towns in the project affected areas.

For establishing small towns, the affected villages may be grouped in units suitably and each unit may consist of 15 to 20 affected villages covering a population of 35,000 to 40,(00. In each small town all facilities for the urbanised social life would be provided.

Along these small towns the CIDCO or the State Industrial Development Corporation will establish industrial growth there. As suggested earlier the Industrial Training Institutes will run courses in these small towns. The other courses may also be run there. The trained people either will be absorbed in the jobs or they will be encouraged to run their own small industries, workshop, trades, *etc.* by giving them financial and other assistance. In these small towns employment exchanges be opened to cater to the needs of the affected people. The City and Industrial Development Corporation and the State Industrial Development Corporation will encourage the local entrepreneurs as well as those from outside to run their industries here.

The artisans such as carpenters, blacksmiths, shoe-makers, goldsmiths, tailors, brick-makers, potters, leather tanners and producers of other articles may be encouraged to form their own cooperative societies through which their problems of finance, raw-materials and marketing of produce will be solved. The cooperative movement will also have a role to play in these small towns.

These arrangements will provide income from non-agricultural sources as well as urban living to the affected people. The problem of allotting land from the command area will not arise in cases of affected people who have been provided with non-agricultural sources of income. Those affected people who may not fall in this category will be free to purchase new land for cultivation. They may be allotted land from the command area. They will also have an opportunity to run other urban occupations.

A difficulty inherent in establishing small town may be that the village people may be reluctant to lose the identity of their respective villages, and hence may not be much willing to merge their identity in the small towns. They are traditionally rooted in rural life and in the beginning they may find it difficult to adjust to the urban living. But this problem may be tackled by moulding the public opinion through public education. The City and Industrial Development Corporation in the State of Maharashtra has rigorously moulded the public opinion through propaganda while establishing twin city near Bombay. Therefore, this matter may be left to the City and Industrial Development Corporation.

The downtrodden people face the problems in rural area. If these people are exposed to the urban living, it is hoped it would help in bettering their socio-economic conditions in these small towns. So it would be an added advantage of these small towns.

10

Rehabilitation and Relocation : Theory and Practice

Mohammed A. Kalam* and V. Sudarsen*

All through history groups of people, communities and populations have moved from one place to another of their own volition or because they have been forced to do so. In the former case, there is no stress, strain or discontent. On the other hand, when a population is relocated the process that is involved brings to the fore quite a few unforeseen processes. Relocation of people and attempts at rehabilitating them have gone on, universally, for generations. However, it is quite surprising that not many significant studies have been made which could have facilitated the development of a general theory of relocation and rehabilitation. Before we examine such a theory let us first decipher the reasons for relocation of populations. Though in general relocation is confined to rural and hinterland areas it is also possible that at times urban populations could also be moved from one urban area to another or as more often happens from an urban area to the

*Department of Anthropology, University of Madras, Madras--600 005

outskirts or periphery of a city. As of today, most attempts at relocation are more or less in rural areas, ostensibly for the exploitation and development of natural resources. On the other hand, relocation in urban areas is entirely for a different purpose : it is either for the clearance of slums and ghettos or for the so-called city beautification attempts. Sometimes this is carried to such ridiculous lengths that even fishermen who have been living on the coast for hundreds of years along with their boats, kattamarans and nets are considered to be eyesores for the tourists and the general public.

Though the main concern of this paper is the relocation and rehabilitation of people as a result of developmental processes, nevertheless, let us also deal with the people affected in urban areas.

According to Chambers :

> Large-scale efforts to develop a region or a country are often linked to attempts to improve an area's ability to capitalise on its natural resources--whether through the construction of dams, the exploitation of forests and range lands, the mining of precious minerals, or the development of fuel. Almost invariably these projects affect prior users of land where the resources are found and have a significant impact on people who live in the area. In many cases, as in the construction of dams, human populations have to be resettled before resources can be effectively exploited. In other cases, as in the development of fossil fuel resources an area that was previously only sparsely settled may experience a radical influx of population. In still other instances, such as in the conversion of forest to agricultural uses, one population group might be replaced by another. Sometimes, the mere presence of a resource innovation such as the construction of nuclear power plant, might have a significant impact on nearby human settlements even though no great changes in population distribution are anticipated (1985 : 84).

The efforts narrated above have been on for quite sometime and there is every likelihood of these efforts increasing day by day as demands for more returns in terms of energy and power will lead to further exploitation of the natural resources and fuel fossil resources. Cost of enregy resources is increasing and attempts at alternative resources are being made and these in turn will have an impact on the flora and fauna and the overall environment itself.

Given the fact that requirements of human groups can be anticipated, it should be possible to plan out much in advance the kind of project that is to be implemented, and it should be possible to foresee the kind of impact that the implementation of such projects will have on the area in general and the human population in particular. Moreover, having observed similar processes elsewhere it should be possible for the planners and the bureaucracy to consult the social scientists and anticipate the kind of reaction and response that they are likely to encounter. Unfortunately, hardly ever are such studies undertaken. As such, it is not surprising that the resistance that has come across in rehabilitation and relocation programmes is quite hostile in almost all cases.

Scudder and Colson, based on their long term work in Zambia's Gwembe Valley and their participation in policy related projects in other parts of Africa, have been able to delineate certain general observations as to how people who are being relocated react. Scudder has also been able to generalise a "relocation theory". He says "rural communities undergoing compulsory resettlement respond in the same general fashion irrespective of their socio-cultural background and of the policy of resettlement authorities" (Scudder and Colson : 1979 : 246). The response, Scudder feels, is one of "extreme stress".

Scudder and Colson argue ;

> In coping with this stress, relocated communities behave as if they see socio-cultural systems as closed systems, a response which greatly facilitates prediction by the anthropologist. They cling to familiar people and familiar institutions, changing during the initial years following removal no more than necessary to come to terms with the new habitat including its prior habitats. Presumably because the level of stress is close to a critical threshold, radical

changes from within (revitalisation for example) and from without (including attempts by planners to change social organisation) are rejected (1979 : 247).

Commenting on the above argument Chambers says :

> Scudder and Colson suggest that resettlement schemes, no matter how culturally sensitive or imaginative, will probably not have much impact on the way people respond to forced removal from their homeland. This may seem like an extremely negative conclusion with little value to the decision maker faced with implementing a resettlement programme ; but we need to consider that a major objective of public decision-making is to arrive at accurate assessment of the relative benefits and costs of particular plans of action. Scudder and Colson's conclusions respond to this level of policy articulation. Decision makers must consider such evidence in their planning, and the human cost of any project involving such resettlement should be calculated at a higher ratio to its assessed benefits. By the same token, we can see how the promise of a rational and humane resettlement plan could erroneously be added to a calculation of benefit and used to underestimate the actual human costs of forced relocation. In either case the knowledge based on which such assessments are made has the potential for tipping the scale as to whether dams are built, highways are constructed or other resource innovations are attempted (1985 : 85-86).

The foregoing argument of Chambers is based on his observation that '...both private and public decision makers have become increasingly sensitive to the human costs often associated with resource development. In many countries government regulations and laws require that an assessment of project impacts on human populations be included in the process of deciding whether to proceed with a particular development scheme" (1985 : 84). Unfortunately, in India decisions are made on the basis of political whims and fancies and not by assessing the "actual human costs of forced relocation", in spite of the fact that with past experience it is definitely possible to chalk out future relocation programmes in an imaginative and sympathetic manner.

While dealing with relocation and resettlement let us also throw some light on those urban groups who have increasingly become prone to relocation. Almost all major metropolises have a housing problem due to which large sections of populations the world over have to make a living by taking shelter in the so-called ghettos and slums. Without going into the reasons for the origin of such living areas, which anyway are by now very well known, let us look at the feasibility of the highly trumpeted "slum clearance programmes".

Unless there is a drastic change in the planning and implementation spheres of housing the slums are here to stay. Whenever attempts were made to do away with slums there have been broadly two kinds of consequences : one, unimaginable human suffering due to large-scale demolitions and the forcible relocation of people far away from the cities, and, two, the changing of the structure of the slums—from its erstwhile horizontal existence to the newly "designed" vertical ones. In the former case the slums within the city limits were considered to be "eyesores" and hence, they had to be obliterated : in their place sprang up multi-storeyed complexes and sky scrapers for the urban rich. In the later case multi-storeyed structures were built for the slum dwellers themselves and this was thought to be the way of getting rid of the "dirt and filth". But invariably it so happened that the planners succeeded in just turning the horizontal "problems" into vertical ones. Moreover, in most cases it was not thought of as to how these dwellers on the *terra firma* could accommodate their cattle, poultry, fishing nets, *etc.*, in the newer habitations. As a consequence most such multi-storeyed structures were either rented out and sublet or just abandoned. In some cases as in St. Louis these high rise structures had to be dynamited.

Harris explains as to how it came about :

To avoid charges of coddling the poor for whom this huge high-rise project was built in St. Louis, elevator exits were installed only on alternate floors and water pipes

> were run through the corridors. Vandals broke the corridor windows, the pipes froze and burst, water cascaded down the stairwells and then froze. This rendered the stairwells unusable and trapped hundreds of people on alternate floors in waterless and heatless apartments. Plagued by vandalism and crime and unable to obtain funds for security and maintenance, the housing authority decided to dynamite the buildings and level the entire project despite the acute shortage of low income housing (1985 : 386).

We have to examine as to why attempts are made to clear slums. It is mainly because the neighbouring and surrounding, relatively rich sections of the population do not want the slums to be around. On the other hand, what do the slum dwellers themselves want ? Basic sanitation and health facilities with the availability of portable water. Past experience has shown us that it is well-nigh impossible to "clear" slums. At best, we have to settle down for the improvement of the minimum needed facilities in such areas. Given the above, to what extent is it justified to have organisations and committees named as "Slum Clearance Board" and "Slum Clearance Authority". Is it not time to change these to ' Slum Clearance Board" and "Slum Clearance Authority"? The basic question involved here, as we see it, is not of providing a "shelter" and thereby going in for cosmetic changes, but it is a very wider issue concerning the distribution of and access to wealth and assets. Unless a structural change takes place in our society, we do not see how such superficial, half-hearted and cosmetic efforts are going to bear fruit.

Sometimes it is argued that relocation (of all kinds, tribal, rural and urban) and the consequent rehabilitation will help and enable the relocatees to join the "national mainstream", and bring about national integration. Such reasoning is quite thoughtless and at times disturbing because of ideological questions that are involved. We are still grappling with the nature and character of secularism that we are supposed to be practising ; very few people subscribe to the kind of secularism that was advocated by Jawaharlal Nehru. He believed in the total divorce of religion from politics and pleaded for the development of a scientific temper. On the other hand Mahathma Gandhi held a diametrically opposite view as regards secularism which in any way was not as disturbing or dangerous as that of some fundamentalists of today. We would like to emphasise again that it is more important to think of and work towards the achievement of egalitarian goals rather than beseeching the tribals, minorities and similarly placed groups to join the national mainstream.

To sum up, whether it is the issue of relocation and rehabilitation or anything else that affects a group of people it is important to work out the cost-benefit analysis of a project not just in financial terms but a heavy premium is to be placed on the disturbance and suffering that is going to befall the affected population. Consequently, we feel a project is not worth it if it is going to cause a heavy damage to the environment and as a result affect the present and all future generations to come. As we have argued earlier, with hindsight it should be possible to devise relatively foolproof schemes and projects and thereby mitigate human suffering. Of course when we deal with human beings it is difficult to work out fail-safe mechanisms ; but sincere, sympathetic and well thought out schemes should go a long way in lessening the misery of the populations that are under the threat of relocation.

REFERENCES

CHAMBERS, E. (1985) *Applied Anthropology : A Practical Guide.* Englewood Cliffs : Prentice-Hall, Inc.

HARRIS, M. (1985) *Culture, People, Nature : An Introduction to General Anthropology*, New York : Harper & Row.

SCUDDER, T. and E. COLSON (1979), "Long Term Research in Gwembe Valley, Zambia," in *Long-term Field Research in Social Anthropology*, eds. G Foster, *et al.* New York ; Academic Press.

[illegible] very early [illegible] from [illegible] pointed [illegible] By the [illegible] remains. On the other hand [illegible] [illegible] [illegible] [illegible] [illegible] of relatives [illegible] change [illegible] [illegible] [illegible] [illegible] [illegible] [illegible] [illegible] [illegible] [illegible] [illegible] groups [illegible] [illegible]

[illegible] [illegible] [illegible] [illegible] [illegible] [illegible] [illegible] [illegible] [illegible] [illegible] [illegible] [illegible] [illegible] [illegible] [illegible] [illegible]

[illegible]

11

Displacement and Rehabilitation : Issues for Policy Planning

R. Siva Prasad*

Major interest in rehabilitation studies emerges due to the impact of rehabilitation on socio-economic, psychological, political, ecological and other factors and on the society, at large. Rehabilitation studies provide a critical outlook of rehabilitation policies for planners and policy makers. While they are important for planners and policy makers from the policy and implementation point of view, they are relevant for the academics to understand the changing socio-economic scene, which is essential to programme welfare measures in order to ameliorate the affected population. Their relevance for reformers, voluntary organisations, social workers and philanthropists, whose chief concern is to improve the lot of the displaced, only enhances their importance.

Rehabilitation is a multi-faceted and long drawn process. It involves an incisive understanding of the problems involved

*Consultant (Sociology), Om Consultants (India) Pvt. Ltd., Bangalore.

and requires proper planning. It needs the co-ordinated effort of specialists from diverse disciplines, voluntary and philanthropic associations, social workers, officials and active participation of the affected population. In this regard, involvement of voluntary associations is important from two angles :

(1) they can act as pressure groups to extract the maximum benefits for the displaced, and
(2) they can act as liaison between the displaced and the government (Punalekar, 1984).

Basically, rehabilitation is an aftermath of various factors, *viz.* natural, political, social and developmental activities. It is essential to note that there exists a basic relationship between the process of rehabilitation and the causes of displacement. Thus it becomes essential to understand the causes of displacement for a realistic planning and programming of rehabilitation.

II

Based on the causes, rehabilitation activities could be broadly grouped into five categories :

(1) displacement due to natural calamities,
(2) displacement due to political, racial, religious and other related upheavals,
(3) displacement due to development activities,
(4) displacement due to social inequalities (weaker sections), and
(5) displacement due to physical and psychic factors (handicapped).

Among these five categories 1 and 2 have a general similarity in terms of their sudden nature, to some extent unanticipated, of displacement. Though there are fundamental differences between these two, both require some period of relief before actual rehabilitation. In the case of displacement due to development activities, displacement of persons will be known much in advance and planning for rehabilitation could be made and implemented well ahead of the actual displacement. Hence, any failure of rehabilitation in such cases may be attributed directly to the lack of proper planning (Karve and Nimbkar 1969 : 10 ; Maiti 1978 : 14).

The displacement due to social inequalities poses a different set of problems for rehabilitation. The weaker sections such as Scheduled Castes, who have suffered traditionally at the hands of caste Hindus, need economic and social rehabilitation. Here, although the rehabilitation activity has some similarity with earlier categories, the emphasis is on specific social groups. The last category, *i.e.* the displacement due to physical and psychic factors is mainly concerned with the rehabilitation of the handicapped. This rehabilitation activity, unlike the others, is at the level of individuals only.

III

It may be relevant here to delineate broadly the nature of problems of the above five categories of rehabilitation. In the first category, the forced evacuation due to earthquakes, floods, conflagrations, severe famines, *etc.*, could result in a greater amount of physical and economic losses for which the evacuees may not receive adequate compensation and immediate relief. The evacution could be temporary or sometimes permanent. Primarily, relief is required in terms of food, clothing and shelter, and secondarily, permanent rehabilitation. The gap between relief and rehabilitation may not be long and they may have to be undertaken simultaneously. Further, in most of the cases, the affected may not be completely removed from their natural habitations. The rehabilitation activity should involve not only the reconstruction of social, cultural and economic life but also include measures to prevent their future occurrence.

The displacement of people due to political, social, religious and other allied upheavals mostly uproot them from their cultural bases to a totally different cultural milieu. They could all be broadly termed as 'refugees'. Rehabilitation of refugees needs a different approach compared to the others. As in the earlier case, refugee rehabilitation also has little scope and time for prior planning and hence, needs relief activity. Unlike the earlier one, refugee rehabilitation requires a long period of relief. In fact, the gap between relief and rehabilitation will be longer in the case of refugee rehabilitation than in any other type of rehabilitation. In addition, refugee rehabilitation requires proper understanding of their social, cultural, economic, educational and occupational background. This would provide a basis for better planning of rehabilitation activity and also helps in its successful implementation.

The developmental activities initiated during the post-Independence period in India, under successive Plans, in the backward regions, by starting large industrial complexes, nuclear, thermal and hydro-electric power projects, major irrigation projects, *etc.* have resulted in large scale displacement of people from their native villages. These people are forced to sacrifice their interests and sentiments attached to their traditional villages, houses and lands in the larger interest of the society and nation. Hence, it is the bounden duty of the authorities concerned to provide housing, land, basic amenities, infrastructural facilities, *etc.* to the oustees and settle them in new areas. This requires a well orchestrated planning. Since rehabilitation planning is possible much in advance, an attempt should be made to improve the living conditions of the oustees. However, the period of rehabilitation and impact of rehabilitation depend on proper execution of the plan and provision of amenities and infrastructure facilities.

The rehabilitation of weaker sections and handicapped are totally on a different footing, in that, the affected population is not really removed from their natural settings.

Our chief concern in this paper is to evolve a package programme of rehabilitation planning, with particular reference to oustees, which could be adopted all over India uniformly. In order to evolve a uniform programme of rehabilitation, it is essential to identify positive and negative aspects of rehabilitation. While the negative aspects throw light on the drawbacks and limitations and provide a cautious approach to rehabilitation programming, the positive aspects give us the plank on which we can initiate the programmes with confidence.

IV

It is to be noted here that though the causes for displacement are different, the experience of rehabilitation has been more or less similar, from the points of view of both the displaced as well as the government. Generally speaking, refugee rehabilitation programmes are better planned and executed than the rehabilitation programmes for the oustees. In other words, in the case of the former there is uniformity in rehabilitation policy while in the latter there is none. This is not to imply that the rehabilitation activity is smooth and satisfactory with the refugees.

Even though the rehabilitation programmes for the refugees are well planned, the cultural dislocation, problems of assimilation, long stay in the relief camps, emphasis on wrong priorities by the authorities or rehabilitation planners, have resulted in tardy progress of rehabilitation (Barnow 1966 : Maiti 1978). The preferential treatment given to the refugees, and the total neglect of local population, has also created social tensions between the refugees and local residents who are mostly poor. This shows that there is a need for amelioration of the lot of the local people along with the refugees and pave the way for a better relationship between them.

The lands allotted to the refugees were not properly developed for cultivation, which only meant additional burden on the already crippled refugees. Elsewhere, lands distributed were government lands meant for distribution among the weaker sections. This implies that not only the rehabilitation of the weaker sections was delayed but in some cases virtually abandoned :

This brief discussion on refugee rehabilitation brings into focus the following issues needing proper attention of rehabilitation planners :

(1) development of rehabilitation locations before actual allotment and occupation ;

(2) differential emphasis respecting socio-economic background of the affected ;
(3) understanding cultural and socio-economic structural factors of the affected as well as the locals for helping better assimilation of the affected with the locals ;
(4) agro-ecological aspects for the success of rehabilitation programmes ; and
(5) necessary assistance, guidance, motivation and creation of gainful employment for the rehabilitation planning and provision of necessary infrastructure.

V

While refugee rehabilitation brings out some shortfalls in rehabilitation planning, the rehabilitation of the oustees indicates yet another set of problems. It is relevant to note that establishment of major industrial complexes or developmental activities like resettlement of shifting cultivators, *etc*. have affected mostly the tribal populations and weaker sections (Vidyarthi 1970 ; Money 1977 ; Muthayya *et al* 1984 ; Karve and Nimbkar 1969 ; Hasan *et al* 1983).

Before undertaking any rehabilitation programme, it is necessary to convince the affected population on the imperative need for their shifting to new centres. Utmost caution is needed in planning and execution of shifting the oustees, avoiding use of force or coercion (Shatrugna 1981). The process and programme of rehabilitation should be on the principle of persuasion. In other words, the first task is to psychologically prepare the oustees for the task through education and with emphasis on positive aspects of the project. Secondly, it is essential to involve the oustees, especially those belonging to weaker sections, small and marginal land-holders, in the planning and implementation of rehabilitation activity. Finalisation of rehabilitation centres should be done in accordance with the needs of the affected population. As far as possible, the oustees should be shifted *en bloc* and to areas closer to their old settlements.

Differences in socio-economic background have a bearing on varied experience of rehabilitation. It is to be noted that the poor are generally the victims of displacement and subsequent rehabilitation. This holds true with the tribals also. It has been the experience everywhere that rehabilitation generally leads to a decline in income and increase in the size of landless agricultural labour, resulting in marginalisation of the affected population. The experience in rehabilitating the poor and members belonging to weaker sections will be completely different from the rehabilitation of the rich and upper caste members. Thus an understanding of the socio-economic background of the population and their problems due to displacement and subsequent rehabilitation would be very useful for a better formulation of rehabilitation programmes. Further, this suggests that differential emphasis should be given a consideration based on the socio-economic background of the affected in the rehabilitation programme.

It is necessary to check the veracity of the land records before initiating the valuation of lands for paying compensation. This is essential to eliminate the possibility of wrong persons receiving compensation for the land, while the right persons are left in the lurch. This implies an effective legislation to discourage absentee landlordism.

Enough land should be procured for purposes of rehabilitation. In order to do this, the slab should be fixed in such a manner that from each family in the rehabilitation region some area of land is acquired. (Usually big landlords resort to division of families to project themselves as below slab and holders in order to avoid land acquisition). In order to quicken the process of land acquisition, it is necessary to simplify land acquisition laws and procedures. The offices concerning rehabilitation and land acquisition should be located closer to the affected villages. Besides, there should be only one officer to deal with land acquisition and rehabilitation in an area. This would be convenient for all the affected to contact only one officer for all related matters. Further, co-ordination of rehabilitation activities under one body would be essential for both uniform implementation of the programmes and monitoring the progress. It is also necessary to simplify the procedures that are cumbersome in the entire process of rehabilitation.

In order to achieve a greater success in rehabilitation

planning and its execution, the entire organisational machinery should be geared up in such a way that there would be better co-ordination and smooth functioning among various agencies involved in implementation. As far as possible red-tapism should be avoided for a speedy implementation of the programmes. In general, at every stage of the rehabilitation activity proper representation has to be given to the oustees—poor, landless and weaker sections, and marginal and small farmers—for achieving better results and also to satisfy the oustees.

It is necessary to remember that no compensation should be paid in cash in the very beginning of the rehabilitation process itself so as to prevent the displaced from squandering away the money. Instead, it is essential to develop the rehabilitation centres by providing necessary infrastructure, amenities, *etc.* and by building houses for the affected population. This would not only save the money on rehabilitation but a planned change would be possible to improve the quality of life. It is important to note that the traditional patterns of life should not be drastically altered as it would lead to a large scale resentment of the affected and this might lead to the failure of the rehabilitation activity itself. The responsibility of shifting the population to the rehabilitation centres should be shouldered by the authorities and every possible assistance has to be provided to the shifting households.

As in the case of refugee rehabilitation, family identity cards may be maintained. In these cards particulars regarding social, economic, educational and occupational background of the oustees have to be recorded for the purpose of proper rehabilitation. This would eliminate the chances of others misusing the benefits of rehabilitation, as usually happens in the case of new migrants. These cards should be updated annually. This would not only facilitate to review the situation, but also to keep track of the development taking place.

Compensation should be given in terms of land to land, house to house, *etc.* Agricultural lands should be, as far as possible, closer to their settlements. Even in cases where compensation is paid in cash, it should be paid at once and not in instalments. At the time of paying compensation, deduction of loans to banks, co-operative society *etc.*, and towards small savings should not be resorted to, as it defeats the whole purpose of paying compensation for rehabilitation. Further, when compensation is paid, it should be adequate enough for the oustees to purchase similar assets elsewhere. Besides, when compensation is paid, it should be ensured that the oustees purchase productive assets. Compensation should be paid not only for the lands and houses, but also for the trees on the lands. While assessing the value of property, both lands and houses, the authorities should also include non-officials in estimation committees, preferably from the oustees, voluntary agencies, philanthropists, lawyers, engineers, *etc.* This would minimise the problems of litigation and, in turn, short-circuit the delay in rehabilitation activity.

In order to ameliorate the conditions of landless and the weaker sections, at least 5 acres of agricultural land and 5-8 per cents of house sites which could accommodate livestock should be given to each household. Mere lands would not be sufficient and they should be properly reclaimed and developed before they are distributed to the oustees. When the lands are given to the oustees, they should be given permanent rights (*pattas*) over the lands so as to avoid any future litigations. They should be given loans, on easy instalments basis with less interest, to develop their lands and to revitalise the economy. It is also necessary that suitable cropping pattern, taking the local practices into consideration, has to be evolved and the oustees need to be persuaded to follow them for better returns. The entire planning process should take the local value system into account in planning crop systems, residential colonies, *etc.*

In case the government is not in a position to provide land to all the land-owning households those who are not given lands should be employed either in the project or in any other government enterprise commensurate with their capabilities.

In case the government is not in a position to provide land to all the land-owning households those who are not given lands should be employed either in the project or in any other government enterprise commensurate with their capabilities. While providing employment, weightage needs to be given to the landless and weaker sections. Besides, oustees should be given guidance and training to start new ventures and they may be given financial and technical assistance for this purpose. During the period of training some stipend or scholarship should be given. The Government should start some industries, especially agro-based, in order to develop the economy of the region and also to absorb the local population by generating employment. Private enterprise also has to be encouraged in this regard.

As in the case of refugee rehabilitation, it is necessary to treat a family with more than seven members as two units for the purpose of rehabilitation. In cases where a family consists of more than one married couple, each one should be treated as an independent unit. This should be taken note of when the house sites are allotted to the oustees. In order to avoid any conflict between the locals and the oustees, some of the benefits given to the oustees, other than land and house sites, should also be extended to the locals, especially to those belonging to the weaker sections. At the time of construction of houses contract for constructing houses should be given to the oustees themselves, in terms of 'labour contract'. This would not only provide employment but would also develop the feeling of involvement and would minimise the costs of rehabilitation. A similar thing should also be done in the case of land reclamation and development and other activities. This would immediately provide an alternative source of employment and facilitate acclimatization of the oustees. Also, this would give a breathing time to rehabilitation programmers to plan the alternative occupational structure.

In cases where forest land is cleared for accommodating the oustees, steps have to be taken to maintain an ecological balance. Social forestry may be encouraged in this regard. For the success of rehabilitation programmes in general, and revival of the economy in particular, agro-ecological aspects of the region have to be considered in planning the local economy, crops, livestock employment, *etc.*

Rehabilitation experience shows that the success of rehabilitation programmes also depends on the locational advantage of the rehabilitation centres (Gajarajan 1970). If the rehabilitation centres are well developed or linked by communicational network, marketing facilities *etc.*, and if sufficient land is available, it can accelerate the pace of development. As a step in this direction, model small towns should be planned as market centres. These model towns can also ease the problem of rehabilitation, apart from developing the entire region. In order to take care of the heterogeneous character of the regions, different strategies have to be adopted for different regions. Further, to minimise the socio-psychological effects of rehabilitation, new settlements have to be named after the old villages. As far as possible, social and climatic conditions should be similar.

In order to avoid speculation in land, a strict check on selling and buying of land should be there to prevent outsiders from buying land at low prices and later raise the prices, thus leading to a sort of black-marketing in land. In order to remedy the situation, the government should act as a real-estate agent to assist the oustees in buying land. Also, free legal aid should be provided to the oustees in order to eliminate middle-men taking advantage of the situation and to arrive at out of court settlements for compensation.

Since rehabilitation leads to a decline in income, relief should be provided to the oustees at least for a period of three to four years, as in the case of refugee rehabilitation. This would help in stabilising the economy of the oustees, especially of those belonging to weaker sections. In order to bridge the gap between upper and lower castes, the distance between upper and lower caste localities should be minimised. Further, the school building, panchayat office, residences of village officials, police post, *etc.*, should be located in a place central to all the residential colonies. Generally, these are located in the caste Hindu locality, where rich landlords, traders and other high status and caste families live. In order to encourage the oustees to send their children to schools and colleges, education up to college level should be made free and freeships should be given to the children of oustees. Adult education programmes may be undertaken to improve the level of literacy and to remove certain superstitions among the oustees.

It is necessary to note that the Governments have undertaken various developmental programmes in rural areas for the uplift of the poor and those belonging to weaker sections. These should be clubbed with the rehabilitating the affected belonging to the poor and weaker sections. For instance, developmental schemes like NREP, RLEGP, food for work, IRDP *etc.*, should be combined with the activities of infrastructure creation and employment generation programmes.

IV

In summary, the rehabilitation package should give priority to provide alternative agricultural land, residential sites, house in case of poor and weaker sections, civic and social amenities, employment opportunities and monetary compensation for resettling the displaced. In cases where alternative agricultural lands cannot be provided, employment and additional compensation should be given to the oustecs. Emphasis should be laid on developing agricultural lands, evolving cropping pattern, encouraging horticulture, animal husbandry and involvement of the oustees in the entire activity. Oustees should be given developmental loans and also some concessions to the children of the oustees in education and employment. There should be facilities to train the willing oustees in skilled jobs. In general, they should be given relief for a period of three to four years. Overall, put differently, there should be both short-range and long-range planning. The organisational framework should also be designed accordingly.

REFERENCES

BARNOUW VICTOR : (1966). "Sindhis Mercantile Refugees in India : Problems of Their Assimilation". *Phylon* (Atlanta, quarterly), 27 (i) : pp. 40-49.

GAJARAJAN, C.S. (1970). *Planned Rehabilitation and Economic Change : A Case Study of Tungabhadra River Project Rehabilitation Colonies at H.B. Halli.* Poona : Gokhale Institute of Politics and Economics.

HASSAN, AMIR *et. al.* (1983). "Impact of Industrialisation on Displaced Persons : A Study in Mirzapur District, Uttar Pradesh". *Journal of Rural Development 2* (5) pp. 548-59.

KARVE, IRAWATI AND JAI NIMBKAR, (1969). Survey of the People Displaced Through the Koyna Dam (July 1965 to January 1967). Poona : Deccan College.

MAITI, R.C. (1978). "Horticulture to Rehabilitate Refugees in Dandakaranya". *Yojana* 16 : 13-15.

MONEY, K.S. (1977) "Kedaripuram Colony : A Case Study in the Rehabilitation of Shifting Cultivators". Administrator, (*India, Quarterly*), 22 (1) : pp. 319-24.

MUTHAYYA, B.C. *et al* (1984). Rehabilitation of Displaced Villages : A Plan. Hyderabad : National Institute of Rural Development.

PUNALEKAR, S.P. (1984). "Voluntary Action and Rehabilitations : A Case of Narmada Dam Oustees in Gujarat State". ***Indian Journal of Social Work***, 44 (4) : pp. 353-94.

SHATRUGNA, M. (1981). "Andhra Pradesh : Unrehabilitated Poor of Srisailam Project". *Economic and Political Weekly*, XVI (52) : pp. 2123-26.

VIDYARTHI, L.P. (1970) Social-Cultural Implications of Industrialisation in India : A case Study of Tribal Bihar. New Delhi : Research Planning Committee. Planning Commission, Government of India.

12

Displacement and Resettlement : A Conceptual Frame of the Problems and Prospects

A. Xavier Raj* and Satwant Kaur*

Displacement of people has occurred, in a historical sense, at all times in some form or other. During the early stages of human evolution man has been a wanderer, migrating from one place to another perfecting his techniques for survival. The change in living conditions entailing the movement brought about transformation in early man's socio-economic organization and subsistence pattern. Moreover, man had to safeguard himself from natural calamities like floods, earthquakes, and food scarcity ; the only option available to man was to migrate to a new 'safe' place. Where a population was unable to move it perished under the trying conditions. As time passed the causes for displacement became more complex. Invasions,

*Research Scholars, Department of Anthropology, University of Madras, Madras.

wars and conquests triggered off large scale movements of populations. Industrialisation and modernization added a few more dimensions to displacement. And, twentieth century is witnessing massive movements of people, dislocated by war, ethnic conflicts, natural calamities, industrial disasters and implementation of developmental projects. The sheer increase in the number of displaced people since World War II has complicated the problem further.

I

Based on the causes, displaced people can be classified into three categories : first, the refugees and repatriates ; second those who are displaced due to natural disasters like floods, earthquakes, droughts and famines ; third, those who owe their displaced status to developmental process.

The first two categories of displacement are abrupt in nature and under normal circumstances cannot be predicted. As Schechtman has pointed out these victims are "objects rather than free subjects of a given ... situation which is in no way of their own making and which they have no choice but to bear" (Quoted in Keller, 1975). On the other hand, "displacement caused by different kinds of developmental projects are not unforeseen occurrences and hence the extent of displacement can be visualised and provided for" (Reddy, 1989). This fundamental difference apart, each category is distinguishable on legal and administrative basis as well. Nowadays, the legal status of an uprooted person (refugee, repatriate or displaced person) is crucial in determining the type of assistance an individual is eligible to get. While refugees are protected by international conventions, the rehabilitation of repatriates and internally displaced persons is considered the responsibility of the concerned nation state. Often, for political reasons, the international organisations are kept away and the issue is tackled at a bilateral plane by the respective governments. The best example is Sri Lankan Tamil refugees and Sri Lankan Tamil repatriates to India.

The first category, refugees and repatriates, forms the major chunk of the displaced persons in any country. Since the Second World War, with the emergence of new nation states, many new dimensions have been added to the refugee concept. Now, it has increasingly come to signify persons fleeing not only political persecution but also violence, war-like situations and even economic and ecological disasters (Dossier, 1986). The multiplication of causes for refugeeism has also led to increase in the number of refugees. Resources have to be mobilised at global level by international organization for relief measures and rehabilitation of the refugees.

Some agencies distinguish between a 'refugee' and an internally 'displaced person' (DP). The refugee status is accorded to a person who has been uprooted from his home, has crossed international border, and looks for protection and sustenance from a foreign government. In legal terminology, he is a designated refugee, as he lacks the diplomatic protection granted to nationals abroads (Holborn 1968 : 362). On the other hand, the DPs are those who are forced by circumstances beyond their control to leave their homes within the borders of their own country (Stein, 1981). Sometimes the DPs are called "internal refugees"or "natural refugees".

The best examples of internally displaced person can be found in Africa (displaced due to severe drought and warfare), in Central American countries (warfare) and the victims of Delhi riot in 1984 (ethnic conflict). They normally return to their homes once the normalcy is restored. But, like the refugees, they also need assistance for resettling.

Often the plight of DPs is worse than that of the refugees. As the DPs lack refugee status, they do not benefit from UNHCR (United Nations High Commission for Refugees) assistance. Only severe calamity as it happened in Ethiopia, would bring assistance from other countries and international organisations. As most of the victims of economic and ecological disasters and ethnic conflicts are found in less developed countries, the concerned governments find it difficult to organize adequate relief measures.

The second category, the natural disaster victims, can be subdivided into two groups. First is the victims of cyclones, floods and earthquakes. The second is the victims of droughts and famines. The former differs from the latter in terms of experience and the duration of crisis. As the cyclones, floods and earthquakes are abrupt and inflict severe damages to the life and property the victims generally suffer from what is known as disaster syndrome : that state of dazed or stunned blackness (see Keller, 1975). But, the crisis normally affects a section of the population in only one location. Once the crisis passes over, the victims recover quickly and return to their normal life. An individual may lose a relative or his property, but he knows life has to go and overcomes the setbacks in due course. Temporary relief measures are required to treat the injured, camps for housing the victims and monetary assistance to repair the damages.

In the case of droughts and famines, people have adequate warning before the food scarcity situation assumes disastrous propositions. Since, in many areas it occurs periodically, a government can plan in advance and mobilise the resources for organising relief works. In general, temporary dislocations may result, especially those of small farmers and landless labourers moving to other areas in search of work and food. Except a few, most of them return to their villages once the situation returns to normalcy. The disruptions to the social life is minimum and in drought prone areas, the periodic displacement itself becomes a way of life. But it is likely, under severe recurrent drought conditions, the government mechanism may break down and result in large scale exodus to neighbouring regions and countries, creating a refugee situation as it happened in Ethiopia recently.

The third category of displaced people is relatively a new one. These 'new' displaced people are an outcome of colonisation and later the development programmes launched by many newly independent countries. The intentions behind the development planning are laudable objectives of providing food, shelter and other comforts to all the citizens. But the fruits of development programmes do not benefit everyone equally. A section of country's population is adversely affected by the implementation of various developmental projects. Often, thousands of people have to be evacuated to clear the way for the construction of major irrigation and multipurpose projects, mining mineral resources, establishing heavy industries, defence projects, conservation activities, *etc.* On the positive side, it results in overall development of hitherto economically backward area, extension of communication network, increased employment opportunities, increase in per capita income and so on. But on the negative side, it also results in disruption of the well-knit community life, disintegration of traditional institutions and leads to maladjustment in the society (Reddy, 1986), especially those sections of the society which are vulnerable.

Besides, there are also possibilities where a village or group of villages has to be relocated to save the people and cattle from the effects of industrial pollution. But public awareness in this regard is abysmally low. This, coupled with the utter callousness shown in dumping the hazardous industrial wastes may lead to enormous human misery. Often, the people affected live in an isolated village and by the time a decision is arrived at to relocate the people, much damage would have already been done. They are the indirect victims of industrialisation which is a part of the 'development' process.

Another case in point is the plight of tribals being marginalised in their own ancestral land by developmental activities, restrictive forestry laws and conservation measures. The restrictions imposed on the tribal's hunting activities, grazing land available for their cattle and the cycle of shifting cultivation results in severe strain on the existing social and economic organization. Adverse land-to-man-ratio, introduction of new value-system by the non-tribals and the ruthless exploitation by the money-lenders has led to a situation in many areas where the tribals have become homeless wanderers eking out a livelihood under difficult circumstances. This class of people are the indirect victims of the developmental planning and confront the same social, economic and psychological problems of displacement. But their predicament is much worse as they are not covered under any rehabilitation schemes. And, resettlement for this physically and socially uprooted people is a neverending process.

It must be mentioned here that the majority of the people adversely affected by developmental process are firstly the tribals and secondly the rural poor. By coincidence the tribals happen to be sitting on top of rich mineral, oil and forest resources

(Kalam, in press). As the tribals are main forest dewellers they constitute the multitude of those displaced by dam construction as well. They have little understanding of the forces responsible for their rehabilitation. But frequently they get a raw deal from the government and if the resettlement and relocation occurs, "they lose their ancestral lands, their source of livelihood and their cultural heritage – forever" (Nachowitz, 1988 : 25). Similarly the small farmers and landless labourers are affected by the inadequate compensation they receive from the government. The beneficiaries of relocation and resettlement are the wealthy landlords and they receive major chunk of the compensation. As they stand to profit from the relocation they support the relocation and resettlement. The small farmers, though they do not want to leave their ancestral lands, fearing police action they meekly submit to the wishes of the big landlords (Nachowitz, 1988).

II

Any displacement is a source of social change. It is possible to say that for the displaced people the time span of normal social change is compressed (see, Saklani, 1984). Displacement of people from their familiar environment disrupt their social, economic and cultural organization. The complete severance, physically and culturally, inflicts considerable psychological distress. The psychological trauma they undergo has profound impact on their adaptation to new physio-cultural environment. Rapid transformation results, with changes in social, economic political, ritual and psychological aspects of the uprooted. They have to make compromises at different levels and surmount many obstacles. Many realise after having gone through the traumatic process of displacement and their ordeal is not over but it is only the beginning. The success in finding decent livelihood depends on many factors which will be discussed in the subsequent pages.

III

The degree of harm done to the social and cultural fabric of the refugees is substantial compared to other categories of displaced people. The refugees are completely uprooted from their homes and cultural moorings. The dislocation severely affect their traditional life-style. Important social, religious and community functions are postponed due to social and economic constraints. In course of time, they adopt some ritual aspects of ceremonies, value system and life-style of the local community.

In the case of repatriates, it is a kind of home coming, after a period of stay in a foreign country. Under normal circumstances, as they would be setting in a familiar physical and cultural environment they are not expected to have much of an adjustment problem. But often this is not the case. If the period of stay outside the country is long enough, then they also face similar problems encountered by the refugees. One good example is that of Sri Lankan Tamil repatriates settled in India.

While the disruption of social life is immediate for refugees and repatriates, it is not so for those displaced due to developmental projects. In most of the cases the disorganization occurs over a period of time. As the displacement is part of a planned programme, the villagers are aware of the impending resettlement. Though they do not want to be uprooted from their ancestral lands, they wait endlessly for their resettlement. As the construction activity begins, they are exposed to new winds of ideas, values and life-styles. This initiates the social and economic transformation which ultimately strikes at the well established norms, customs and traditional community organization. In some cases, resettlement may act as a trigger to set off many dormant undercurrents leading to the fissioning of the community into two or more groups.

Cultural dissimilarities between relocated (especially the refugees and repatriates) and the local population is another crucial factor which further complicates their process of resettlement. It is true that in any kind of displacement, the victims normally tend to settle in close proximity to their place of origin; neighbouring country or region. But the massive dislocations in Africa, Asia and Latin America have initiated a new trend whereby many of these refugees are settling in Europe or North America. "They are culturally vastly differ-

i
wo
ing
burea
roach.
should
the peop
involvemen
Special atte
orphaned chi
training and edu
ted people fron
process. The mai
ression should also b
The disruption ca
But special efforts shou
weaker sections of th
absence of adequate reh
deprivation and misery.
recurrent phenomenon, gov
employment to the landless la
should be augmented with tra
ammes which would enable th
higher level of self-sufficiency. In
care must be taken not to disrupt th
Here the target should be the rehabil
munity not of an individual.
The displacement of people as a cons
lopmental projects is intentional and
approach. There is sufficient time to c
community-specific rehabilitation schemes.
standing in conceiving the rehabilitation sche
per implementation have deleterious impact o